THE
American
Retail Value
Proposition

THE
American
Retail Value
Proposition

CRAFTING UNIQUE EXPERIENCES
AT COMPELLING PRICES

KYLE B. MURRAY

UNIVERSITY OF TORONTO PRESS
Toronto Buffalo London

ISBN 978-1-4426-3717-7

Printed on acid-free, 100% post-consumer recycled paper with vegetable-based inks.

Library and Archives Canada Cataloguing in Publication

Murray, Kyle B. (Kyle Bayne), 1973–, author
The American retail value proposition : crafting unique experiences
at compelling prices / Kyle B. Murray.

Includes bibliographical references and index.
ISBN 978-1-4426-3717-7 (hardback)

1. Marketing – United States.   2. Retail trade – United States.   I. Title.

HF5415.1.M87 2016   658.8'700973   C2016-901907-1

University of Toronto Press acknowledges the financial assistance to its
publishing program of the Canada Council for the Arts and the Ontario Arts
Council, an agency of the Government of Ontario.

**Canada Council
for the Arts**   **Conseil des Arts
du Canada**

ONTARIO ARTS COUNCIL
CONSEIL DES ARTS DE L'ONTARIO
an Ontario government agency
un organisme du gouvernement de l'Ontario

Funded by the   Financé par le
Government   gouvernement
of Canada   du Canada   Canadä

To Colleen, Julia, and Lilly

Brief Table of Contents

Part 5: Putting It All Together

Detailed Table of Contents

Foreword

In the classic movie *Field of Dreams*, Kevin Costner's character is haunt-
ed by a voice that instructs him repeatedly, "If you build it, he will
come." The magic of the film is, of course, that the prophecy proves
true, and the ghost of his father does arrive.

Seemingly, many of the retail propositions we see in the market today follow a similar philosophy – though in their case, the collective
"he" is the consumer, supposedly thrilled to arrive at the store and to
play in the aisles.

But how can retailers successfully take this approach when they have
to operate under some of the most dynamic yet challenging market
conditions in history? The permanence of online retailing and ongoing
new technological innovations involving digital promotions are changing the face of retail forever. Combine this unceasing technology with
the increasing global nature of retail and the competitive pressures it
brings, and merchants are hard-pressed to create a sustainable value
proposition. The retailer's field of dreams is more a field of battle, and
with Target and Walmart, rue21 and Lowe's expanding their presence
both online and offline, emerging merchants are finding it harder to approach the consumer in a way that doesn't simply revert to fighting a
market-share war where the common weapon is price.

Little seems to indicate that the course will change, and it is easy
to be distracted by all the channels and technological innovations. Today's retailer is, after all, faced with an ever-evolving and increasingly
competitive environment where consumers have unparalleled power
and use mobile phones to check prices, and where products are readily
available from online specialty merchants that can compete on the basis
of ease and assortment.

Against this formidable backdrop, Kyle Murray reinforces with wonderful clarity that at its core, successful retailing is still about the customer. It is about developing a carefully crafted strategy to address that customer's needs, and then executing precisely against this strategy across the many dimensions available to the merchant. Starting with a clear line of sight on the customer and then adopting the fundamental principles embodied in Murray's ESE model of environment, selection, and engagement, any retailer should be able to fully express the brand experience it wants in order to support its strategic purpose.

And, as Murray illustrates, this brand strategy can be designed to realize the lifetime value of the customer.

An early mentor of mine once advised that the power of a great strategy is as much about knowing what you are **not** going to do as it is about knowing what you **will** do. As someone who has worked on the frontlines with retailers, I know that sometimes this lesson gets lost in the heat of competition. Remaining relevant to the consumer and developing a value proposition beyond price is the only way to create a sustainable and defensible competitive position in the market. True, few retailers are lucky enough to have the product leadership of an Apple or a lululemon, but these retailers post some of the highest sales per square foot not only because they have unique products, but also because they have developed a full experience that supports and embodies their brand. This is territory that is available for any retailer to exploit.

Many merchants may wonder, then, where and how customer loyalty figures into this mix. Being in the business of loyalty programs myself, I find it entertaining when executives are surprised to find that their customers usually rank their loyalty program below the fourth or fifth item when asked to rate why they shop with that particular retailer.

From my perspective, that's the way it should be, since a loyalty program should never be viewed as a replacement for a sound and competitive value proposition. When the retailer pays attention to every feature that shapes the consumer experience, from store location and design to the interior signage and the specific merchandise that lines its shelves, it is giving respect to the environmental and selection components of successful retailing. And while loyalty does play an important role in building customer engagement, as a practitioner I can't help but agree with Murray's views. Loyalty programs are an important way to connect with customers via rewards and recognition, but the real value of any program is in its ability to bring customer data to bear on the business, shaping all of its operations. The knowledge gained by understanding the customer at a more granular level will help any retailer shape and continually improve its strategic approach.

As Murray points out, we need to build brands around *customers* – rather than just products – since the ability to create powerful relationships with consumers will be the key to building a powerful retail brand in the future. In a clear and effective manner, *The American Retail Value Proposition* will help retailers move beyond a pure merchandising mindset to a fuller understanding of what it takes to launch or refine a retail brand in today's hyper-competitive environment – one where price seems so key, but where customer experience may well define the winners and losers of the future.

If retailers build the customer's experience around the principles of Murray's teaching, then I can't help but believe that yes, the consumer will come.

Bryan Pearson
CEO of LoyaltyOne

THE
American
Retail Value
Proposition

PART 1

An Introduction to the Retail Value Proposition

Chapter One

Crafting Value

Ron Johnson told Steve Jobs that Apple's retail stores were all wrong. On their way to a weekly planning meeting Johnson argued that the stores were too focused on products. He believed they should be built around the customer experience. The products weren't important; it's what people do with those products that matters. If people looked to Apple for music and movies, then the stores should reflect that. A few minutes later they arrived at the meeting and although they were only months away from opening the first location, Jobs announced to the team that Johnson was going to lead a rethinking of Apple's store design.

By the end of the year Apple had expanded to twenty-five locations in the United States. Within two years, retail operations had surpassed $1 billion in annual sales. Apple stores' sales are astronomical at more than $4,500 per square foot, far greater than other retailers.[1] Landlords actively recruit Apple to their malls and retail spaces around the world. People line up in the hope that they can join the ranks of the "Geniuses."

In hindsight the tremendous success of Apple's stores may seem inevitable. Initially, however, analysts and critics were quite skeptical about the company's potential as a retailer. They believed that a manufacturer running small stores with limited inventory, a heavy reliance on e-commerce, and a non-aggressive approach to sales would struggle in the ultra-competitive electronics market. Nevertheless, Johnson's vision for a new type of retail store proved to be a runaway success.

On the strength of that success Johnson was recruited away from Apple to take over as the CEO of JCPenney. Revenues at Penney were in decline, having fallen from $19.9 billion in 2006 to $17.2 billion in 2011.[2] The stock price followed. Johnson was hailed as a savior who would help modernize and turn around the struggling department store business. Reporter Jennifer Reingold, at *Fortune Magazine*, described the hire "as if a triple-A team had just signed Babe Ruth." After watching Johnson's innovative approach to merchandising at Target and revolutionary store design at Apple, industry observers were anxious to see what Johnson would do for Penney's. The plan was a radical one that came in two major parts. First, the stores would be redesigned with a higher-end atmosphere that would feature a collection of in-store boutiques and fewer private label brands (which historically were an important part of Penney's sales). Second, it would move away from deep discounting and constant price-based promotions. Adopting the disdain of Steve Jobs for market research and concept tests, Johnson moved forward to put his plan into action within three months. Late in January 2012, the day after Johnson's vision was made public, the stock jumped from $34 to $41.

Customers were less impressed. By May 2012, quarterly same store sales fell 19 percent and traffic was noticeably down, even though the company was spending heavily on new advertising. In April, 19,000 employees were laid off. By the end of 2012, JCPenney had lost $1 billion and the stock price had dropped to $18.[3] Johnson's reputation had taken an even greater hit, and less than eighteen months after he was hired the board accepted his resignation.

Retail is a tough business.

Big Hairy Audacious Retailing

In retrospect it is easy to blame Johnson for setting overly ambitious goals to rapidly change a business that was more than 100 years old with 1,100 stores and 159,000 employees. Yet, this type of goal setting is quite common in retail. Walmart, Starbucks, Walgreen's, and many other legendary retailers sparked enormous growth by setting seemingly unattainable goals.

In *Built to Last*, James Collins and Jerry Porras argue that this type of aggressive corporate target – which they name a big hairy audacious goal (BHAG) – is a powerful mechanism for stimulating progress. When stated clearly, such goals can focus organizations that have already achieved a dominant position within the marketplace. By definition, BHAGs appear to be arrogant and impossible to reach. Such goals push already strong organizations to envisage greatness and to achieve what has never been done before.

The classic example of a BHAG in retailing is Sam Walton's statement in 1990 that Walmart would reach $125 billion in sales by the year 2000. At the time, Walmart was already the largest retailer in the United States with about $30 billion in annual sales. The only corporation with sales near $125 billion was General Motors. To reach his goal, Walton predicted that Walmart would need to double the number of stores it operated and dramatically increase the revenue produced in every square foot of every store. The fact that the U.S. economy was in the midst of a recession that had many retailers wondering about their survival made this goal even more audacious. Nevertheless, the company not only reached its target but did so two years early, in 1998. Today, Walmart sits at the top of the Fortune 500 list of companies with global revenue that is nearing half a trillion dollars. No other retailer has sales of more than $200 billion (although Apple is getting close).

Another memorable example comes from Starbucks, which in 1994 set the audacious goal of opening 2,000 stores by the year 2000. Starbucks had only 400 stores when it announced this to the public, which meant it would have to expand by 500 percent in six years to achieve its goal. The business press quickly recognized how exceptional such growth would be, and labeled it the corporate equivalent of Kennedy's plan to put a man on the moon.[4] Setting this goal pushed the already dominant coffee chain to completely rethink and redesign the process it used to build and open new stores. The resulting "mass customization" approach reduced development time from twenty-four to eighteen weeks and cut the cost of a new store from $350,000 to $290,000. By the year 2000, Starbucks operated 3,500 stores. The design changes the company made to the new stores, in an effort to achieve its audacious goal, resulted in savings of about 18,600 operating weeks and $186 million.[5]

Legendary Performance

Putting a man on the moon, growing a discount retailer into the world's largest corporation, and selling coffee for $5 a cup were all ridiculed as impossible goals; but, once achieved, they became the stuff of legends. With the benefit of hindsight, we can analyze the factors that led to success, the best practices that emerged, and the vision that propelled each organization toward these celebrated accomplishments. However, such phenomenal performance is by definition an outlier. For every Walmart and Starbucks, there are an untold number of big retail dreams that never materialize. For every Sam Walton or Howard Schultz, there are countless managers – some very good and some very bad – who never become household names. Why, then, would a retailer set such an outlandish goal when the most probable outcome is failure? To some extent, such BHAGs are ego-driven and supported by the belief that growth is truly limited only by ambition and imagination.

To a greater extent, they reflect an underlying reality of the industry: retailing is an outrageously competitive business that requires organizations to constantly innovate to survive. This is made worse by the fact that retailing is also highly transparent. What one organization does in a store today is visible to the competition before tomorrow. Great ideas are easy to copy, and sustainable competitive advantages are difficult to find. At the same time, the stock market and industry analysts relentlessly push for faster growth and improved profitability on a quarterly, if not monthly or weekly, basis.

In setting big, audacious goals, retailers hope to focus, motivate, and engage their employees to achieve more. Such goals force organizations to look for improvements even when they are already well ahead of the competition. Starbucks, for example, was under no real threat from its competitors and could easily have opened another 400 stores in six years doing what it had been doing. However, it would not have been motivated to rework its store development process, which allowed it to extend its market dominance while saving hundreds of millions in development costs. If Starbucks had set a more sensible or reasonable goal, it is unlikely it would have achieved such extraordinary growth in such a short period.

Of course, both Starbucks and Walmart have also seen difficult times with lagging share prices and slower growth. Aiming at, or even achieving, an improbable goal is not enough to secure long-term success. Setting an audacious goal is not a strategy; it only establishes a direction. For the retailer, it is much more important to understand how those goals can be achieved.

This book is about crafting a retail value proposition and unleashing a company's potential to achieve its most ambitious goals. This is not a simple task. It is a process of strategic planning, implementation, experimentation, and, ultimately, reinvention in an ongoing quest to satisfy customers and stand out from competitors. Successful retailing begins with a strong foundation in the basics of understanding customers and building stores and grows into more sophisticated approaches to product, price, and customer portfolio management. Each part of this book details the individual components that, in combination, become a retail value proposition and determine a company's ability to attract consumers and generate sustainable profitability. Whether you are an aspiring merchant or an industry veteran, the following chapters provide a strategic core from which to build your business. First, however, it is important to understand the pivotal role that the retail industry plays in shaping our economy and our society.

The Engine That Drives the Economy

In the highly transparent and ever-changing retail marketplace, the desire for faster growth, more revenue, and greater profitability creates an atmosphere of intense competition. By setting an audacious goal, Walmart signaled to Kmart, Sears, and others that it was going to fight for every customer relationship, every piece of real estate, every dollar of sales, and every advantage. Such extreme competitive positioning has tangible benefits. From the consumer's perspective, it means that retailers are working hard to lower prices, improve convenience, provide superior service, offer a better selection of products, and enhance the shopping experience. For shareholders and employees, it offers the potential for an enhanced return on investment and greater career opportunities. Society in general benefits from a strong retail industry.[6] Our economy is profoundly dependent on the success of our retailers and the confidence of our consumers. Yet media, business books, and business schools tend to under-value the critical role of professional retail management.

The importance of the retail sector to the global economy is particularly evident during times of crisis. World leaders, faced with a severe economic downturn, look to consumers for help. After 9/11, U.S. President George W. Bush asked Americans to carry on with their lives, not to lose confidence, and to continue spending. Leaders made similar pleas in response to the global recession that began in 2008 and is still having an impact in many parts of the world, because when consumers stop buying, the economy grinds to a halt. In contrast, when consumers are confident and spending freely, money flows through retail stores, up the supply chain, and all the way back to the manufacturers, miners, drillers, farmers, and other producers, making stops along the way with lawyers, bankers, accountants, consultants, and other service firms. Governments pick up their share through corporate, land, income, and consumption or sales taxes. Consumers are at the heart of all of this economic activity.

On an annual basis American retailers sell more than $3 trillion worth of goods and services.[7] That means that on an average day, consumers in the United States are spending more than $8 billion! They buy groceries, automobiles, gasoline, clothes, electronics, drugs, sporting goods, and a whole lot more. These products are sold by dozens of different retailers competing for the same business.

Consumers want to maximize the value they receive for each hard-earned dollar they spend. But value is not just about price. After a long day of traveling, a consumer might find great value in a $4 glass of Coke and ice delivered to her hotel room, while at a neighborhood grocery store, she might baulk at paying $4 for a six-pack. Another consumer might happily pay $2,000 for a suit from his favorite fashion apparel retailer but switch grocery stores to get the lowest price on a loaf of bread.

Retail is the part of the economy that is closest to the customer's wallet, and so it is important to understand how value is created and sustained from the perspective of consumer decision makers. In this book, I provide a framework to address whether a retailer is offering the right kind of value to the right customer at the right time, and explain how to both craft and evaluate retail value propositions.

The Retail Value Proposition

The world's leading retailers create value for their customers by crafting unique experiences at compelling prices. *The Retail Value Proposition* is organized around three principal components that retailers employ to design and manage the customer experience: environment, selection, and engagement (ESE). This approach is built on more than a decade of research into what makes a strong retail organization. It combines insights from academic research with knowledge gleaned from hundreds of conversations with retail executives, store managers, and employees. This book has a consumer-centric bias. My focus is not on the supply chain or human resources or finance, although these issues are important and I touch on them because they affect the value proposition indirectly. Instead, my focus is on the strategic management of *value as the consumer perceives it*.

Perceived value is a combination of the consumer experience the retailer creates and the price it charges in return. But *prices do not create value* – they only capture it. Well-designed retail value propositions that include a carefully crafted shopping environment, product selection, and customer engagement strategy result in customers who are happy, even eager, to pay the asking price. Therefore, pricing strategies should encompass the value consumers perceive in the retailer's goods and services. In other words, great retail value propositions find the right balance between the ESE components and the retail price (figure 1.1).

Below, I introduce the organizational framework for this book. I begin with the basics of understanding the customer and tailoring the shopping environment to the specific consumers the retailer would like to attract. I then discuss the strategies and tactics behind filling that environment with products that appeal to the target customers and engaging those customers in profitable long-term relationships. In the last part of the book, I address the critically important process of pricing in retail marketplaces and conclude with a chapter on the complexity of bringing it all together. In the next few pages, I provide a general overview of the key components of the retail value proposition that I extend and examine in detail throughout the remainder of the book.

Environment

Environment refers to where the consumer shops. To understand the where, it is crucial to identify the who – that is, the first step in crafting a unique retail experience is understanding the customers the store aims to attract. This begins with the basics of market segmentation, target selection, and positioning. Used correctly, this information provides a foundation on which retailers make subsequent decisions about the shopping environment, including the retail format, store location, store layout, design elements, atmospherics, use of technology, and integration across multiple channels (both physical and electronic).

Great retail value propositions make it as easy as possible for consumers to find the products and services they want to buy. The consumer's comfort and convenience are fundamental to the design of retail environments. Over the past several decades, the global standard of living has continued to rise. Part of the cost of greater wealth is a corresponding increase in the time pressure people feel in their day-to-day lives. Consumers prefer to shop in an environment that does not add to the stress of their daily routine. They want the store to feel like a comfortable place and the shopping process to be as convenient as possible. I focus on the store environment and examine the key elements of building a differentiated shopping experience in the first section of this book.

Figure 1.1 The Retail Value Proposition

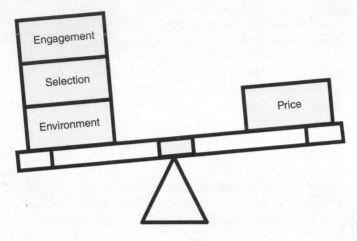

Selection

The convenience and comfort of the retail environment are critical determinants of the store choices consumers make and the quality of the shopping experience. The retail environment can dramatically affect how consumers feel about their time in the store, which in turn can influence spending, loyalty, and word of mouth. Yet ultimately, most retail environments are built for buying – that is, the environment is simply the context in which consumers buy products and services. I address how retailers manage the products and services they offer for sale in the second section of the book.

To begin, good retailers understand that it is easier to sell what people want than it is to convince people to want what you sell. As is the case when creating a compelling environment, managing product selection requires the retailer to have a deep understanding of what the customer wants. In the selection section of this book, I examine the key strategic elements of the retail supply chain and explain how successful retailers get products onto their shelves and how they manage categories within their stores. To understand selection, it is important to have a sense of the buying process, the evolving nature of category and shelf-space management, and fashion and trend management. In this section of the book, I also address the rise of private label brands and their impact on relationships between manufacturers and retailers within the supply chain.

Engagement

Over the years, retailers have become significantly more sophisticated in the tools and techniques they use to create shopping environments and manage their product selections. As a result, it is increasingly difficult to generate a sustainable competitive advantage on these factors alone. In fact, many retailers now believe that the future lies in the past: delivering an intimate local shopping experience. Competition today is less about differentiation through store formats or products and more about the relationships retailers establish with their customers. These relationships are built on the foundation of an inviting environment and an appealing selection, but this foundation is only the beginning. In the fourth section of the book, I focus on engagement and build from basic theories of customer satisfaction and relationship management to address the emerging techniques and technologies that allow retailers to apply analytics to retail management. I emphasize that it is more important to build and maintain a solid base of loyal customers than it is to constantly fight to attract customers away from the competition.

Retail Pricing

After creating an offer the retailer believes consumers perceive as valuable, the next step is to quantify that value and decide on a price. For many organizations, this is the most difficult part of the planning process, yet it remains absolutely critical in the consumer's decision-making process. Ask for a price that is higher than the value the customer perceives in the offer – and damage sales. Sell products for less than the customer is willing to pay – and dilute profitability. In the fifth section of this book, I tackle the problem of pricing directly, beginning with basic microeconomics principles and cost-based methods before moving on to more advanced topics in value-based and dynamic pricing. I emphasize the behavioral science behind how customers respond to retail prices and the critical role perceived value plays in consumer decisions.

Measuring Success

My focus in this book is on creating a compelling value proposition that combines the ESE components to craft a properly priced and clearly differentiated customer experience. An essential element in the development of such a proposition is having the tools to evaluate its success (or lack thereof). I integrate metrics for measuring performance into the discussion of each of the ESE components. As a starting point, I look at the big numbers: revenue and profitability.

When Sam Walton announced his audacious goal for Walmart, he explicitly identified a revenue target of $125 billion. Whether or not the company achieved that goal was easily evaluated in terms of sales. But what about profitability? No business wants to grow revenue without some prospect for future profitability. Even in the early days of the dot-com craze, when companies like Amazon burned through billions of dollars to establish their brands and build their operations, investors bought into the future earnings potential they believed each business possessed. In Amazon's case, investors remain more than willing to support the company's long-term vision. Owners and investors want to see a company grow, but they want that growth to include the prospect of a solid return on investment. On one hand, there is no profitability without revenue. On the other hand, retailers that generate revenue without profitability are unlikely to survive for very long. Profitability says a lot about how consumers view a retailer's value proposition. As the perceived value of the offering increases, consumers are willing to pay more and the retailer has pricing power. When the value of the offering is low, the retailer is forced to lower prices to buy sales. For this reason, revenue growth, profitability, and profit margins – the ratio of profit to revenue – are critical indicators of retail success.

Ultimately, sustainable growth in profitability is the impetus behind investing in a compelling retail value proposition. In the following chapters, I outline the key components that retailers combine to create value for consumers. Each component comes with its own set of metrics to track progress and measure success. Nevertheless, in a for-profit business, these metrics are only signals and signposts that alert the vigilant manager to aspects of retail performance that can impact the ultimate metric: profitability.

Predictably, retail competition continues to grow and become increasingly fierce. For the most part, a dollar spent at one store means a dollar not spent somewhere else. Consumers' dollars are migrating to those retailers that offer the greatest value. This book is about creating that value.

Chapter Two

Segmentation and Differentiation

When the Liquor Control Board of Ontario (LCBO) announced it was adopting the Air Miles Rewards program, pundits baulked. Why would a monopoly retailer selling a product as much in demand as alcohol need to pay a third-party organization like Air Miles to create loyal customers? Critics argued that the LCBO should be able to thrive as long as it stocked its products at reasonable prices. After all, where else could customers go?

In fact, for the LCBO, joining the Air Miles program was not about rewarding customers for their loyalty. Instead, it was part of a comprehensive repositioning that aimed to improve the value delivered to customers.[1] The LCBO is a chain of liquor stores owned by the government of the province of Ontario, Canada. It is one of the world's largest buyers and retailers of alcohol, with more than 630 locations and annual sales of about $5 billion. The company's customers were deeply dissatisfied, and their unhappiness fueled a rapid rise in cross-border shopping and illegal alcohol sales, which market analysts estimate cost the LCBO nearly $1 billion per year in lost revenue.[2] In addition, the provincial government was feeling growing pressure to make changes and was seriously considering privatizing the booze business.

It was clear that being the dominant retailer selling a great product at a good price was not a sufficient value proposition. Customer engagement and the shopping environment were equally, if not more, important. The LCBO's CEO, Andrew Brandt, recognized that the retailer was underperforming in this regard. He described the shopping environment as "extremely hostile and uninviting," and argued that the stores needed to evolve to better serve their customers.[3]

The real value the Air Miles program added was not in the rewards that the LCBO gave to its customers; it was in the data that the customers gave to the LCBO. That information, combined with survey results and census data, helped the company understand how to serve its customers better. It allowed the company to build stores that customers enjoyed visiting in places where customers wanted to shop. Even though the LCBO was the dominant player in the market, it realized that it needed to craft a more complete retail value proposition driven by a deep understanding of its customers. As Brandt explained, "In retailing, in merchandising and in promotion, you better find out where your customer wants to go; what it is your customer really wants from you. Then get out in front of that parade and lead it."[4]

Market Segmentation

When retailers talk about adding value by getting to know their customers, they are talking about market segmentation. When a retailer crafts a value proposition, it should not be meant for everyone. Creating value is about understanding which customer segments the retailer can most profitably serve and focusing resources on those targets.

A century ago, a local general store owner would have known all of his customers personally. He would be familiar with their families, their businesses, where they lived, how they spent their leisure time, and what they were interested in spending their hard-earned money on. This type of marketing is called one-to-one, because the retailer was able to think and act in terms of individual consumers and their households.

Although technology is making it easier for firms to gather customer information and learn what it is that consumers really want, few retailers can get to know all of their customers on an individual basis. Moreover, it is not always necessary to know individual customers, because in many markets there are large groups of consumers who are very similar.

The purchase of ketchup is one example. Imagine that we were to classify every individual American based on what he or she wants when buying ketchup. Given unlimited resources, we could talk to each household and learn about their ideal version of the condiment. We could record their buying habits, conduct surveys, and facilitate focus groups. We might even spend time in consumers' homes to observe how, when, and why they use ketchup.

Ultimately, the return on that investment is unlikely to justify such in-depth market research, simply because consumer preferences are not that unique for many products. Some may want ketchup that is a little sweeter, a little spicier, produced by a particular brand, and so on. Based on a few key features of the product – such as price, quality, and brand name – we can create groups of Americans that care about the same things and base their buying decisions on the same factors. Maybe we find that most people fall into one of three camps: Segment A (price-sensitive) buys primarily on price; Segment B (tasters) buys primarily on taste; and a small Segment C (organics) wants ketchup made from organic ingredients. We could dig deeper and develop a more fine-grained model of Americans' ketchup preferences – for example, exactly how price-sensitive Segment A is, what flavors really make a difference to Segment B, and how much more Segment C is willing to pay for organic ingredients. Ultimately, how far we break the market into groups with distinct preference profiles depends on whether or not investment in more detailed segmentation schemes justifies the additional cost. As it turns out, the ketchup market is largely homogeneous – most people prefer the taste of Heinz 57, and that preference drives their purchasing behavior.[5]

Good market segmentation means finding potentially profitable groups of customers who prefer particular combinations of product attributes. Once a retailer knows what customers want in the products they buy, it can talk to manufacturers and wholesalers to see what products are available and how closely they match the needs of those individual segments. However, as in the LCBO example, most retailers realize that having the right product at the right price is not enough. Modern consumers' needs and desires go well beyond the basic products they purchase. For example, many consumers want the sense of confidence that comes with buying familiar brands. They tend to prefer to shop in a comfortable and convenient environment. Some consumers may want to patronize only retailers that reflect their personal values, through initiatives such as local community involvement or environmental and social responsibility. In other words, people do not just prefer certain products – they prefer entire processes of meeting their unique individual needs. The ability to understand those needs on a segment-by-segment basis is the foundation of a successful retail value proposition.

Segmentation Variables

In practice, retailers tend to begin the market segmentation process by looking at consumer *demographics*, which include variables such as age, income, gender, family size, and life cycle. For example, Toys "R" Us might segment its market based on life cycle and target key groups such as families with young children and grandparents. In doing so, the retailer can build its brand and tailor its message with these groups in mind. It can then focus its marketing resources on the consumers its research has identified as the most (potentially) profitable, rather than broadcasting a generic message to all Americans regardless of their interest in toys. Retailers that operate in other product categories will find value in different demographic variables. For example, a luxury retailer such as Prada or Hermès might segment the market by income and target its advertising toward consumers who can best afford its products.

Retailers also tend to rely heavily on *geographic* information and, in particular, information about who lives in the area surrounding current or potential stores. This information can influence decisions as general as whether to enter a country or as specific as which unit to occupy within a shopping mall. Most retail is still conducted in physical brick and mortar stores, and so geographic data can be especially critical. A store's location tends to define the types of customers it attracts. Geographic data can inform decisions that range from micro-level strategies such as whether or not a downtown neighborhood is appropriate for an Aldi grocery store all the way to macro-level strategies such as whether Target should enter into or exit from Canada. In chapter 3, I further explore the application of demographic and geographic market segmentation to selecting store locations that most effectively serve the target clientele.

A third type of variable marketers use to segment consumers is *psychographic*, which includes consumers' personalities, interests, activities, and values. Dick's Sporting Goods, for example, is a chain of stores built on serving its customers' interests in sports. Barneys New York caters to customers interested in fashion and luxury apparel. Nespresso aims to sell its coffee pods and machines to people who want quality espresso that they can make conveniently at home. Although this type of information may be more difficult to acquire than geographic or demographic data, psychographic information can often lead to a deeper understanding of why consumers make the choices they do, beyond how old they are and where they live. In the engagement section of this book, I address the use of psychographic information in retailers' efforts to better understand their customers.

Behavioral variables make up a fourth set that commonly segments markets and includes when customers shop, how loyal they are, how ready they are to make a purchase, and how frequently they visit the store. For example, the AAdvantage loyalty program allows American Airlines to offer a different value proposition to different customer segments depending on how many miles they fly in a year. Being a member of the Gold, Platinum, or Executive Platinum segments does not depend on age or income (demographics), how much customers like flying (psychographic), or where they live (geographic). It depends only on customers' actual behavior – that is, how many miles they fly. To continue the example from above, it may make the most sense for retailers such as Prada and Hermès to target market segments that buy luxury brand fashions, regardless of income or other demographic, geographic, or psychographic characteristics. In Part 4, on engagement, I dig deeper into how retailers can acquire and use behavioral data to improve both revenue and profitability.

Four Criteria for Evaluating Market Segmentation

It is relatively easy to use the four sets of variables described above to segment a market; however, finding groups that can drive revenue and profitability is substantially more challenging. Ultimately, demographic, geographic, psychographic, and behavioral variables are only proxies for what a retailer really wants to know – that is, which market segments offer the greatest potential return on investment.

To evaluate the results of a segmentation process, retailers should consider four key criteria:

1 *Are the segments clearly differentiated from each other, while clearly similar internally?* Marketers call this out-group heterogeneity and in-group homogeneity. This is an important criterion because if the individuals within each segment are not similar – for example, in their needs, wants, preferences, values, and so on – then it is difficult to tailor an effective value proposition that appeals to the entire group. Similarly, if the segments are not sufficiently distinct from each other and the rest of the market, it is not clear that it is worth investing in the development of a unique value proposition for each group.

2 *Are the segments accessible?* In some cases, the segmentation process identifies groups that are not easy to reach directly. For example, many retailers want to target the most affluent American households. Of course, so do a variety of other organizations and, as a result, those households can be very difficult to reach directly. It makes little sense to craft a value proposition for inaccessible market segments.

3 *Are the segments sizable?* The answer to this question depends on the size of the retailer and its ambitions. A small specialty boutique might need fewer than 1,000 total customers, in which case segments of a couple of hundred people might be sufficiently large. In contrast, Walmart cannot afford to focus on segments of one hundred customers because it serves millions. Although in theory focusing on individual customers allows retailers to provide the most customized products and personalized advice, the potential return on investment should always play a prominent role in determining how finely grained a segmentation scheme will be.

4 *Do the segments have distinct response profiles?* Even when the first three criteria are met, a segment is not of much value if its individual members respond to the same offer in many different ways. For example, a start-up company might find that some people prefer sweeter ketchup, while others prefer a saltier flavor. Its research could even pick out niche segments that like ketchup with maple syrup or habanero chilies. The company may be satisfied that these segments meet the first three criteria and feel it is ready to go to market. However, if the ketchup-buying public opts to purchase Heinz ketchup regardless of their different taste preferences, then they do not have distinct response profiles. Similarly, Best Buy might identify women between thirty-five and fifty as a key underserved segment in the market with considerable buying power. However, that level of segmentation may be insufficient if there are substantial differences in psychographics (e.g., interest within product categories or price sensitivity) and behavior (e.g., some shop in the store only for family members at Christmas and others shop for themselves throughout the year) within that group. Focusing on a very broad market segment may not help the company take any meaningful action that contributes to profitability because that segment is too general and its sub-groups behave in too many different ways. The lack of a distinct response profile can be a strong sign of weak segmentation.

Target Market Selection and Positioning

After breaking a large market up into smaller segments, the retailer's next step is to evaluate the potential value of those segments. The objective is to select smaller groups that offer the greatest potential revenue and profitability. Competition comes into play here. It is important to consider what the company can do relative to the value proposition of other retailers selling similar products or services. There are three criteria to consider when evaluating a company's capabilities relative to the competition and the (potential) target segments:

1 *Are these segments the right targets for now and the future?* This question highlights the fact that segments evolve over time, as does the ability of the company and the competition to serve them. Segmentation, target market selection, and positioning are not one-time projects. Instead, they are ongoing processes at the core of strategic decision making. Nevertheless, although consumers' preferences change over time, most retailers choose to target segments that they expect to be able to serve into the foreseeable future. It is considerably more difficult to generate an acceptable return on investment from market segments that may change substantially in the short term.

2 *How will targeting the chosen segments affect a brand, both within those segments and within the broader population?* In some cases, a deep dive into the segmentation process can obscure the bigger picture. For example, a luxury brand might see an opportunity to grab market share within a price-sensitive segment through aggressive discounts. However, doing so is likely to impact the company's luxury brand image as well as its ability to charge higher prices in other segments. Similarly, a fitness club that chooses to target hard-core body builders might risk alienating the much larger segment of casual athletes. It is important to ensure that strategies targeting a specific segment are consistent with the retailer's overall value proposition.

3 *Does the company have the necessary competencies to generate an acceptable return on investment from the target segment(s)?* This is the big question. There are times when a retailer decides not to target an attractive segment because it lacks the ability to deliver the requisite value. For example, a boutique bakery chain may decide to avoid selling to restaurants that would like to serve its breads because it does not have the ability to produce on that scale. Or the bakery may simply decide to delay entry into the restaurant segment while it invests in the capability to serve those customers effectively. Similarly, a ski and snowboard retailer may see opportunity in selling bikes and skateboards to its customers in the summer but lack the product knowledge and sales staff required to compete with specialized cycling and skating stores. The question of competency is an important one and can be addressed in greater detail by breaking capability into the individual components that are relevant within a particular (potential) target segment.

Differential Advantage Analysis

Imagine, for example, that Rockville Soccer has watched the rapid growth in the yoga apparel market and wants to determine if it could sell similar products within its stores. Rockville is a relatively small chain of five stores in Maryland, Virginia, and the District of Columbia that specializes in the sport of soccer. Assume that it has long identified "soccer moms" as a key target market for a potential extension into the yoga market. The group is unique in terms of geographic, demographic, psychographic, and behavioral data. Further analysis suggests this segment is reasonably large, accessible, and has a distinct response profile. As a target segment, it has good current and future prospects, and putting more effort into serving it is likely to have positive repercussions within the company's other key customer segments. But whether Rockville Soccer can make money in this segment, given the current competitive dynamics within the industry, is still unknown.

A *competitor capability matrix* can help the company address this question. In essence, the matrix lists each of the individual key capabilities in the rows and the major competitors in the columns (see table 2.1). The company then rates all of its competitors on each capability (in this example, I use a five-star scale). This allows Rockville Soccer to assess its strengths and weaknesses within a product category for that particular segment relative to the competition.

This *differential advantage analysis* allows the retailer to decide if it currently has the capabilities required to compete in this market segment. It also highlights the competencies that other companies are likely to rely on to defend their market shares. The capability matrix points out where Rockville Soccer would have to invest to develop the right set of competencies to compete effectively. Integrating the cost of any such investment with the predicted return (e.g., sales and profits) within that segment can extend this analysis to determine whether or not targeting soccer moms has the potential to provide an acceptable return on investment.

To continue with this example, if the analysis resulted in the matrix presented in table 2.1, Rockville Soccer would have to make several decisions before selecting soccer moms as a target segment for yoga apparel. How much will it cost to close the gap in what the company knows about yoga apparel and to build brand equity in that product category among soccer moms? Can the company generate an acceptable profit margin by selling yoga apparel at a competitive price? Is

Table 2.1. Simplified Example of a Capabilities Matrix for Yoga Apparel
in the Soccer Moms Segment

	Rockville Soccer	Dick's Sporting Goods	lululemon
Knowledge of customers' needs in product category	★★★	★★★	★★★★★
Ability to reach and communicate with the segment	★★★★★	★★★★	★★★
Merchandising	★★★★★	★★★★	★★★★★
Product sourcing	★★★	★★★★	★★★★★
Brand equity within the segment	★★	★★★	★★★★★
Cost structure and pricing power	★★	★★★★★	★★★★★
Available shelf space	★★	★★★	★★★★★

it willing to devote floor space to yoga apparel? Would this product category provide a better return on investment than the products currently sold in that space?

Vertical and Horizontal Differentiation

Positioning is about differentiation, which is exactly what a well-crafted retail value proposition should deliver. In some cases, products within a market can be ordered by perceived quality from low to high. This type of market is *vertically differentiated*, and pricing has a strong effect on consumers' preferences among available brands. For example, if the soccer moms segment believes lululemon's yoga products are of higher quality, those consumers will not pay the same price for products from Rockville Soccer that they perceive are of lower quality. In this scenario, Rockville Soccer must either convince the market that its products are of the same or higher quality – an often difficult and risky strategy to pursue – or offer a similar product at a lower price. Vertically differentiated markets tend to have different brand tiers, and as quality increases across each tier, so does price. Positioning within vertically differentiated markets relies heavily on consumers' willingness to pay for quality. In recent years, retailers have introduced their own private label products to create new – and complement existing – product tiers. In fact, brand development and management are inexorably tied to positioning, and I address them in depth in chapter 6.

Another general approach to positioning is *horizontal differentiation* – that is, products that do not differ substantially in terms of how the market views their overall quality or price but instead vary on other dimensions. When a market is differentiated horizontally, products within a category sold at the same price are positioned to attract consumer segments with distinct product preferences. For example, Rockville Soccer might sell a yoga-style pant that works well in the yoga studio but is tough enough for a mom who is constantly on the go driving kids to soccer games and other activities. In this scenario, the portion of the market that wants pants designed for yoga and the everyday life of a soccer mom would tend to buy from Rockville Soccer, while the portion that is not as concerned about everyday wear beyond the studio would continue to buy from a different retailer.

A positioning strategy based on horizontal differentiation takes advantage of the fact that people have different preferences and uses for products within the same category. When pursuing a strategy of horizontal differentiation, retailers strive to identify those segments that differ in ways that affect their buying behavior. Then, as discussed above, the company has to decide if it can make money within that segment. In other words, Rockville Soccer would have to determine if it could generate a good return on investment from soccer moms who would like a yoga-style pant designed for everyday wear.

In practice, most retailers sell products that are differentiated both vertically and horizontally to some extent. For example, to generate interest and gain market share, Rockville Soccer might decide to target soccer moms' desire for a more everyday pant at a lower price than a similar-quality product from lululemon.

Actionable Segmentation and Consumer Personas

Strategies based on market segmentation are only as effective as they are actionable. Even the most sophisticated segmentation scheme, capable of identifying exceptionally underserved and lucrative groups of consumers that the retailer is uniquely positioned to serve, is of limited value if the retailer does not act on it. The LCBO decided to learn more about its customers through regular psychographic surveys and a loyalty program that linked demographic, geographic, and behavioral data, but that information would have been wasted if it had not resulted in a more effective value proposition. In fact, the LCBO used that information to dramatically enhance the shopping environment with new store formats in more convenient locations, a better selection of products tailored to the tastes of individual consumer segments, and an emphasis on better service and customer engagement. The company gained global recognition for its store environments, and the satisfaction of its customers improved substantially.

Making a major organizational change to become a consumer-centric retailer is not an easy task. Solid market research is often left on the shelf or in the filing cabinet as management focuses on day-to-day operations. In other cases, information about the target segments disseminates throughout the organization in a raw form that is difficult to act on. Consider the soccer mom segment discussed above. Imagine that, after a rigorous process of market segmentation, Rockville Soccer decides to target this group of consumers – not just for a new line of yoga pants but as a core group of customers who have a substantial influence over household spending in the soccer products category. The company's research has revealed that soccer moms can be described in terms of the key segmentation variables. It is further supposed that the group ranges in age from thirty to forty-five and has an average of 2.5 school-age children. Segment members have diverse educational backgrounds and higher-than-average household incomes and expenses. Although they can be found in a wide variety of neighborhoods around the country, the company has decided to focus on those closest to its stores in suburban communities. Beyond soccer, soccer moms tend to be interested in a variety of family and sporting activities and are more active than average members of their local communities. They spend a lot of their leisure time at soccer fields and transporting their children to various games, practices, and other events. They are under constant time pressure and put a great deal of value on product quality, helpful service, and a convenient location. Rockville Soccer may even be able to get more specific in terms of how much they spend, what percentage of their soccer purchases are made at its stores, how often they make a soccer purchase, and so on.

In fact, detailed segment profiles can be many pages long and contain a great deal of qualitative and quantitative data. The problem with this type of information is that it can be very difficult to communicate throughout an organization in a way that can be readily acted on. To address this problem, marketers take these profiles and create personas that are easier to work with at all levels of the business. For example,

Rockville Soccer might decide to compress all of its information into "Sarah." Everyone in the organization would then be introduced to Sarah, a suburban soccer mom with a young family and a need for both convenience and superior service.

A good segment persona is one that people within the organization can quickly recognize, with defining features and unique preferences that are easy to remember. Detailed segmentation information should remain readily available for when circumstances require a deeper dive into data, but most of the time the key details are conveyed by simply talking about what Sarah would want. Product assortments and store displays can be built to appeal to Sarah, and employees can be trained to serve her specific interests. Of course, the Sarah segment would have to be integrated with marketing aimed at other key groups, which would have their own unique personas and underlying data that define them. The ease and simplicity of using personas has led many retailers to adopt this approach to ensure they are capable of turning the market segmentation process into action.

Measuring Success

As the LCBO example indicates, even dominant retailers in markets with limited competition and selling products in high demand cannot be successful over the long term by focusing only on products. The remainder of this book is organized around the importance of delivering what customers want in terms of an overall experience that includes the shopping *environment* and customer *engagement*, as well as having the right product *selection*.

This approach begins with understanding the market on a segment-by-segment basis. In this chapter, I have introduced the major variables retailers tend to rely on in their segmentation models and have outlined four criteria they can use to evaluate the effectiveness of a segmentation process. The next step is to ensure that the retailer has the current capabilities to serve the segments identified as the most attractive targets. This can be addressed at a general level by asking the three questions summarized above, or at a more detailed level using tools such as the capabilities matrix. This type of analysis often concludes with a "no go" decision – that is, a company like Rockville Soccer may very well decide that soccer moms are not likely to buy yoga clothing at their kids'store. Avoiding unprofitable segments can be as important as attracting profitable ones.

In this chapter, I have emphasized the importance of return on investment (ROI). This is a critical metric for management decisions. In simple terms, it can be calculated as follows:

$$ROI = (P - C) / C$$

where P is the additional profit that the retailer expects the investment will generate over and above current profit and C is the cost of the investment that aims to generate that additional profit. The retailer can achieve a superior return by lowering costs – for example, because it can spend advertising dollars in a more focused manner to reach a smaller group within the overall population. Or a superior return may be driven by the greater profitability a retailer realizes when it better matches what it offers to what a particular market segment wants to buy. Of course, estimating the profit that will result from a new investment is not always a simple or straightforward task. When the investment is a significant expense, it may be worth conducting a detailed projection of ROI. For example, a retailer might look at multiple outcomes of the investment, including a best-, moderate-, and worst-case scenario. It can then base the decision to proceed on an assessment of the potential risk (i.e., worst-case scenarios) against the prospective return (i.e., moderate or best-case scenarios). This type of analysis can extend to include a comparison between the expected return from an investment in one project (e.g., market segmentation) versus another (e.g., hiring additional staff).

In many cases, the new investment is relatively small and a full-blown examination of the potential ROI is not required. Nevertheless, it is generally worth thinking about the value that can be added by spending more money to better understand one's customers. At some point, the return on investment will no longer justify the incremental knowledge that can be gained from additional market segmentation.

Contemporary retailers make the acquisition and application of customer information a priority, but in practice managers do not have the luxury of complete information. They must make decisions and act on the information available to them. In the remainder of this book, I explain how the world's best retailers use their knowledge about their customers to build compelling value propositions that drive both revenue and profitability.

PART 2

The Shopping Environment

Chapter Three

Locations and Formats

Starbucks is famous for opening stores across the street from each other. The coffee retailer first realized it could operate successful stores like this when it located at 1099 and 1100 Robson Street in Vancouver and those two stores became the top locations by revenue in the entire chain. Years later, in his book *A Double Tall Tale of Caffeine, Commerce, and Culture*, Taylor Clark quoted a former Starbucks executive who explained the importance of location: "Starbucks doesn't have a lockdown patent on the environment; it doesn't have a lockdown patent on the experience; and it doesn't have a lockdown patent on the bean or the roast. All of those things can be duplicated. So what it comes down to is dominance of real estate."

For retailers, the shopping environment is a combination of many decisions, including the store location, format, layout, and design. Increasingly, retailers also grapple with the question of medium – that is, a physical store versus an electronic one. At the core, however, decisions about the shopping environment are not about locations or formats or layouts or channels or media. They are about the customer.

The shopping environment is the context within which customers finalize their purchase decisions and spend their money. It is the place where retailing happens. Selecting that place may be the single most important decision retailers make, because store locations tend to have a major impact on who the customers will be. For example, a pharmacy located in a seniors' center will draw an older clientele, while one located in a suburban strip mall will draw a more diverse suburban one. Location also tells customers a lot about what to anticipate from a retailer. For example, consumers should expect to encounter higher-price retailers when shopping on Rodeo Drive in Beverly Hills, one of the world's most expensive shopping districts.

Location decisions also directly impact retailers' competitive positioning. Over the years, Lowe's and Home Depot have aggressively acquired many of the best big-box locations for home improvement in the United States. As a result, new start-ups or existing businesses looking to expand will be faced with the challenge of finding suitable real estate that is not already occupied by their competitors. In effect, Lowe's and Home Depot have limited the ability of competitors to build stores that could be easily accessed by a large number of customers. Similarly, many retailers negotiate leases with exclusivity clauses to ensure that no competing store can open in the same development. Companies such as McDonald's and Starbucks use this type of lease agreement, in combination with relentless expansion, to get closer to consumers and limit opportunities for the competition.

Convenience

From the consumer's perspective, location is primarily about convenience. If I want a cup of coffee in the middle of Minnesota's winter, I have to be very loyal to Starbucks before I will walk past a Caribou Coffee to get myself a grande latte. When market researchers ask consumers about the most important factor in their store choice decisions, convenience regularly tops the list – not entirely surprising in a society where time is more valuable than money for many people.

Convenience, however, does not always refer to the store that is closest to home. In fact, the most convenient grocery store might not be the one closest to your house but the one on your route home from work. The most convenient dry cleaner could be the one beside your kids' school, and the most convenient restaurant might be the one next door to the movie theater. One-stop shopping can also be a convenient way to buy, even if you have to drive farther to get to the store. For example, for many people Walmart is not the closest discount clothing store, grocery store, tire store, McDonald's restaurant, hairdresser, or electronics retailer. But a single trip to Walmart allows a busy family to visit all of those "stores" at once, which is convenient. In fact, sometimes the most convenient store has no physical location at all. Even though a consumer might have to wait days for the delivery of a book bought online at http://www.barnesandnoble.com, rather than driving twenty minutes to pick it up immediately, making the purchase from the comfort of home can be extremely convenient. Ultimately, convenience is about making it as easy and efficient as possible for customers to complete a purchase, a task that requires a deep understanding of those customers.

The Rise of Retailing

The location decision has always been a fundamental driver of retail success. Many of the most iconic retailers in American history benefited from locations in large and fast-growing cities. In the mid-1800s, it would be hard to imagine a retailer achieving the size and scale of stores such as Marshall Field's, Wannamaker's, or Alexander Turney Stewart's Marble Dry Goods Palace outside of centers like Chicago, Philadelphia, and New York. These stores had to be close to customers in densely populated areas because travel was extremely inconvenient by today's standards. In contrast to modern retail giants, these pioneers focused their efforts on very large single-location stores. This approach made sense given how difficult it would have been to handle the logistics of multiple locations before the telegraph and railroad were well established. Managing the buying process and shipping inventory was a substantial challenge in the early 1800s when a trip between major centers like New York and Chicago took weeks.

By the late 1800s, however, technology was dramatically changing the retail business and opening up new opportunities as the railroad made it possible to transport goods and people over long distances in a short period. The New York-to-Chicago trip could now be completed in a day rather than over weeks, and the telegraph allowed for rapid long-range communication. The catalog businesses of companies like Tiffany's, Sears Roebuck, and Montgomery Ward became increasingly viable for retailers and attractive to consumers. General stores in smaller towns and rural communities were suddenly competing with these larger retailers, which were developing nationally recognized brand names. This competition pushed the retail industry as a whole to improve its value proposition.

By the early 1900s retailers were able to open multiple stores across the country that aimed to serve increasingly targeted individual communities. By the 1930s this led to the dramatic growth of chain retailers like Walgreen's, which ran more than 600 stores, and Piggly Wiggly, which operated more than 2,600 locations!

The leading retailers of today are constantly scouting and evaluating potential new store locations. Sophisticated global supply chains and instant worldwide communication have made it easier than ever to operate stores in a variety of different locations. As a result, the location decision continues to be an incredibly important decision and one that tends to both drive and constrain the potential of individual stores.

The Location Decision

Successfully choosing a store location requires a deep understanding of the customer segments the retailer aims to serve. Armed with knowledge of the chosen target segments, the retailer next needs to map out the geographic areas around the potential store. Specifically, before finalizing the location decision, retailers tend to follow a process that includes the following steps:

1 **Select the general geographic area.** Often it makes sense for a retailer to develop a critical mass in one area before expanding into new ones. For example, a retailer with a chain of stores in Houston and San Antonio will generally be more successful moving a little north in Texas to Austin and Dallas before expanding to Pittsburgh or Seattle. Regardless of the strategy that underlies opening a new store, the first step is to select the general region, province, or city in which that store will be located.

2 **Map the market segments within that area.** Once a retailer selects a general geographic area, the next step is to map out the local market segments. Ideally, the new store will open in an area that contains (or is expected to attract) a high percentage of consumers within the segment(s) the retailer is targeting.

3 **Map the competitors within that area.** After mapping out where the target customers are located, the next step is to map the competition. At this stage, a retailer should consider the level of market saturation – that is, the number of competitors in the area relative to the number of customers being served. Entering a saturated market with established competitors is generally not the best investment of resources. When mapping competitors, retailers should also consider customers' routes of travel and the ease with which they can access the new store relative to those of the competition. In some cases, a retailer also maps its existing stores and considers the potential for cannibalization – that is, any business the new store will take from its existing stores.

4 **Map complementary businesses within that area.** With a good understanding of where the customers and competitors are located,

retailers consider the effects of complementary businesses in the area. Many retailers, for example, like to be located near high-traffic businesses such as grocery stores or in busy malls, especially if those companies tend to draw the retailer's target segments to the area.

In other cases, neighboring retailers can make a new store more convenient. For example, a cheese shop located next to a deli and a bakery is likely to be more attractive to consumers than one located next to a bookstore and a convenience store.

5 Identify and evaluate potential sites within the mapped area. Of the available sites that now remain, the retailer should further narrow the list based on the ability of the site to support the desired store size and format, as well as other considerations such as business licensing and the terms of available leases. Last, but certainly not least, the retailer should conduct a review of the trade area (see below), which defines the types of customers the store is most likely to attract. Each retailer has different priorities when evaluating a prospective site. Depending on the retailer's overall strategy and its strategy for the specific store, it might choose to emphasize one or more of many potentially important factors, ranging from development costs and desired formats to traffic and competition.

6 Finalize the store format. The retailer's desired store format should be integrated into the location decision. Stores meant to serve an urban population have a format and footprint that is distinctly different from those meant to serve suburban or rural populations. Nevertheless, in the process of matching available real estate to retail strategy and target customer segments, the format of the store requires some modification and adaptation.

Trade Areas

A *trade area* is the geographic space from which a store draws most of its customers or potential customers. The location of the store is the focal point within the trade area, and where the shoppers live or work around that store forms the relevant geographic space. A trade area can be defined in terms of physical distance or the time it takes a customer to travel (from work or home) to the store. For high-traffic retailers, it might also make sense to subdivide the trade area into zones of core, primary, secondary, and tertiary shoppers. Some retailers may define core shoppers as the most valuable customers in terms of the number of trips per month and the average amount spent per trip. Other retailers may define seasonal trade areas. For example, a store may have a small trade area composed of core customers most of the year, but that area may expand significantly over the summer months or during the holiday season.

Customer Spotting

There are several different ways to estimate a trade area. The most common method is simple *customer spotting*, which plots customers' addresses on a map and defines the trade area by those plots. This can be done directly or indirectly. The direct method is simply asking customers for their address or postal code. When customers' postal codes are combined with census data, the retailer is able to learn a great deal about both the geographic and demographic characteristics of its customers. The retailer can then use this information to determine how effectively it is reaching the target customers and to update its market segmentation research. In addition, the retailer can use this type of geodemographic data to direct future interactions, such as market research and promotions, toward core customers within the trade area. Postal-code-targeted surveys can, for example, provide supplementary psychographic and behavioral information on trade area customers. Within the constraints of privacy laws, it is also possible for a retailer to indirectly capture some of this information through sales records, loyalty programs, contest entries, and other mailing lists.

Gravitational and Demand Gradient Models

More sophisticated quantitative approaches to estimating a trade area tend to rely on gravitational or demand gradient models. One approach is to use the size of the focal point – that is, the store or group of stores at the center of the trade area – to estimate how far the trade area will reach.[1] This approach can be extended by taking into account the retailer's other stores, as well as competing stores, to estimate the boundaries at which customers are indifferent about shopping at one location versus another.[2] Similar methods allow the retailer to examine where its trade area overlaps with that of the competition and (potentially) tailor its marketing within those areas to reflect the heightened level of competition. These models can also account for the drawing power of both competitors and complementary businesses. For example, when Lowe's and Home Depot build stores right next to each other, they each benefit from an extended trade area, as customers are willing to travel further with the expectation that with two stores in the area they are more likely to find what they need. Similarly, a Costco or a large shopping mall can ·dramatically expand the trade area of other retailers in the vicinity.

Estimating Trade Area Potential

Ultimately, the goal of the process of market segmentation and store location is to maximize the new store's probability of financial success. After identifying one or a small set of attractive sites, the retailer can begin to estimate the sales and profit it expects to achieve. If the company has other stores located in similar trade areas with comparable levels of competition, it can use the existing stores as an analog to estimate the performance of the new store. For example, if similar stores average $500 per square foot in their first year, then that is a reasonable expectation for the new store.[3]

However, if the retailer is opening its first store or entering a new market that is not comparable to its other operations, a more abstract method of forecasting is necessary. To a large extent, such methods depend on the quality of the data available to the retailer. In general, the process involves an analysis of the value of the customer segments within the predicted trade area. In particular, the retailer needs to be able to answer the following types of questions: How many households are in the trade area and to which customer segments do those households belong? How much does the average household in each segment in the area spend within the relevant product categories? What market share does the retailer expect to achieve in each segment? The answers to these questions can be used to calculate an estimate of potential sales:

$$ER = N_H \times AS_H \times MS_E$$

where ER is the expected revenue, N_H is the number of households in the trade area, AS_H is the average amount spent at the retailer per household within the relevant product categories, and MS_E is the individual retailer's expected market share. When the retailer serves multiple segments within a trading area, it can compute ER on a segment-by-segment basis.

Some of these data are available at a general level from the United States Census Bureau (http://www.census.gov/). Additional information can be acquired through market research and, in some cases, specialized consulting firms. Ultimately, as the quality of the retailer's initial market segmentation research increases, so too does the ease of selecting a store location and estimating its performance. Nevertheless, there will always be some missing information and several unknowns when making a store location decision. Retail managers need to be comfortable with and capable of making decisions under uncertainty, learning from experience, and evolving with changes in the marketplace.

Choosing a Store Format

Once the retailer selects the location, it needs to decide what format the store will adopt. Of course, these decisions may also be made in reverse – that is, a retailer may choose a store format and then look for a suitable location. However, that is an increasingly precarious approach as leading global retailers build stores that cater to the local target segments within a particular geography. For example, Target stores vary their architectural designs by region, with Spanish-style stores in California, prairie architecture in Wisconsin, and tropical designs in Hawaii. Retailers that apply a cookie-cutter format to serve unique customers in different locations will find it increasingly difficult to compete with more sophisticated and localized store designs.

The format decision is really about how the retailer presents products and services, and includes the look and feel of the store, the layout of aisles and fixtures, the arrangement of products and categories, and external visibility and signage. Although in theory a store format is only limited by the designer's imagination, to a large extent it is determined by the location and the retailer's budget. Downtown footprints are different from those of suburban big-box stores. Street-level shops in trendy districts differ from stores in mega-malls. However, the target segments the retailer wants to attract should be a key input into its choice of available formats. Ultimately, a store's format should be the physical manifestation of the retailer's value proposition.

Store Size and Layout

A retail store's square footage directly impacts the number of products it can carry and, to some extent, the number of customers it can serve. Over the past couple of decades, stores have increased in size as retailers and consumers embrace new, and often suburban, real estate developments that cluster several big-box retailers at one location. These "power centers" take advantage of lower real estate prices on the edge of urban areas to build bigger stores with larger trade areas. In addition, because these big-box retailers are grouped together, they all benefit from a trade area that is larger than they would be able to achieve individually. Consumers attracted to power centers are generally willing to drive a little farther to shop in exchange for the ability to access a variety of larger footprint stores that offer an expanded selection of products. This style of development has been very successful in recent years, with many of the country's leading retailers using the big-box format to drive growth.

However, such developments are now so common that many retailers believe future growth requires a more diverse portfolio of store formats. Even retailers like Walmart and Home Depot, who pioneered the big-box format, are building stores with smaller footprints to appeal to urban customers who want to shop closer to home. In essence, when a retailer decides to build a larger store, it bets that it can use that extra square footage and expanded inventory to attract the higher volume of customers it needs to generate an acceptable return on investment. In contrast, as retail square footage decreases, so too does the number of products a retailer can carry. Moreover, smaller stores tend to have smaller trade areas and fewer customers. As a result, they have to ensure that the products they carry are well matched to the customers they attract. With limited space, it is difficult to simultaneously appeal to multiple market segments. Therefore, the location decision is especially important and requires the small retailer to emphasize geographic segmentation – that is, as stores get smaller, they generally need to be located closer to the customer segments they target. On the other hand, while larger format stores can carry a greater variety and broader selection of products that appeal to distinct customer segments, they have to attract enough customers from each segment to justify the added cost of that expanded space.

The size of the store also affects its layout. Stores with only a few thousand square feet of retail space (or less) are usually constrained to some variation of the rectangular floor plan, with shelving along the walls and a few fixtures in the center of the store. Larger stores tend to build their product displays into aisles that are often grouped by product category. Although retail stores come in a wide array of layouts, they can be organized into a few general categories. For example, there are the basic rectangular aisles, hub-and-spoke models, and "rack-track" designs. Some retailers use walls or shelving to create an independent space, often referred to as a boutique or store-within-a-store, which focuses on a particular product category or features certain items.

In recent years, retailers have realized that aisle width can have a dramatic impact on how comfortable people feel while shopping. In addition to the obvious value that wider aisles offer to mothers with strollers or seniors with walkers and scooters, consumers like to have more space. For example, in his book *Why We Buy*, Paco Underhill popularizes the notion of the dreaded "butt brush" – that is, when the aisles are narrow, consumers avoid products lower on the shelves so they don't have to bend over and risk having another shopper brush up behind them. Retailers have also learned that what goes on the end of an aisle is an important consideration. Aisle "end caps" grab consumers' attention and allow the retailer to highlight particular products and promotions.

In fact, how store layouts interact with product placement and shelf management is at the heart of most retailers' merchandising plans. The layout of a retail store directs the flow of customers, which in turn directly affects the shopping experience. Moreover, once the environment has been designed, it sets the parameters within which the rest of the retail value proposition can be crafted. I discuss in-store shopper marketing in depth in chapter 4. I further explore the interaction between the store environment, product selection, and customer engagement in Parts 3 and 4 of this book. Specifically, in Part 3, which focuses on product selection, I examine the interplay between the store environment and product category management. In Part 4, I delve into the approaches retailers use to engage customers in the shopping experience, which is itself a function of the store environment and product selection.

Building the Brand: Locations and Formats Define Retailers

The importance of the format decision extends beyond the functional considerations of how many products a retail store can carry, how it presents those products, and how many different customer segments it can serve. Format decisions define retail brands. The unique design of Apple's glass cube store in Manhattan is one example of a format that not only sells products but also sends a strong signal about those products. For Apple, which relies on its image of design and innovation to drive sales and protect its price premium, the dramatic cube architecture in the heart of the "Big Apple" visually reinforces the company's value proposition.

Similarly, when lululemon opened its first store in Vancouver, it chose a street-level location away from malls and big-box developments because founder Chip Wilson wanted to build a retail experience distinct from that of typical apparel chains. He believed that the consumers who have the greatest influence on fashion apparel trends wanted unique alternatives to mass-market locations. As the brand grew and more people became aware of lululemon, the company opened stores in more mainstream retail developments. Nevertheless, a big part of building the right brand image was the selection of the location and format of those early stores.

In fact, many iconic retail brands are inextricably linked with their locations. From its mermaid logo to its familiar green color, the Starbucks brand is closely connected to the company's first location in Seattle's Pike Place Market. Similarly, Walmart was created in the small town of Bentonville, Arkansas, where it still maintains its head office.

One of the best-known examples of the connection between real estate and retailer is the story of Marshall Field's: "The store that helped build Chicago."[4] Shortly after it first opened its doors in the early 1900s, Marshall Field's was widely recognized as the world's leading department store. It was famous for being a pioneer in sourcing a wide variety of products from global locations, including American sewing machines, Russian furs, Japanese screens, French gloves, and South African diamonds. It displayed those products on mahogany and glass fixtures and offered them to customers by means of more than two thousand in-store sales people.

However, beyond product, service, and location, the store is best remembered for the way it changed retailers' beliefs about what was possible in retail format design. Although it has been more than one hundred years since Marshall Field's first opened its doors, the "Marshall Field's shopping experience" has rarely been equaled. The store was enormous even by today's super-center standards, with more than 750,000 square feet spread out over thirteen stories. When it opened, it had twelve entrances and fifty elevators, which were all jammed full of customers as more than 500,000 people visited the store during its first week in operation.

Marshall Field's Chicago store continues to be revered for its innovations in internal design – what today's retailers call *atmospherics*. At a time when many people traveled by foot or horse-drawn carriage, a strong unpleasant odor often characterized urban shopping. In response, Marshall Field's was one of the first retailers to put perfume

counters at the store entrances and to display fresh cut flowers throughout the building. Music was also an important part of the early environment: six orchestras serenaded shoppers as they traveled through the
store. The architecture remains a Chicago tourist attraction. Although
Marshall Field's was taken over by Federated Department Stores in
2005 and rebranded under the Macy's banner, the State Street store is
still fondly remembered as "the landmark building with its towering
marble columns, Tiffany mosaic dome and twin great clocks that has
represented the best in Chicago for over 100 years."[5]

The legends of Marshall Field's, Starbucks, Walmart, lululemon, and
many other iconic retailers serve as vivid reminders of the power of
store location and format to define retail brands. Store designs can create a wide variety of experiences that range from luxurious to exciting
to soothing to simply efficient. The key to success is integrating the environment with the rest of the value proposition.

Measuring Success

Location and format decisions reflect the intersection between available
real estate, target segments, retail strategy, competition, and sustainable
profitability. Often, the ultimate decision is a compromise between the
ideal and the available. In the United States, mall stores, big-box stores,
and urban street-level stores are still dominant. Nevertheless, many
alternative formats also play an important role in the industry. These
include everything from farmers' markets, which have become small
retail incubators, to e-commerce portals, to pop-up retail stores that aim
to make a large splash in high-traffic locations over a short period.

Retail real estate choices result in significant investments that are not
easily changed in the short term. While many aspects of retailing – such
as product selection, merchandising, employee training, advertising,
and so on – can be adapted and revised in the short term, locations and
formats tend to have more enduring effects on revenue and profitability. For large retailers – some of which open multiple new stores every
day – real estate decisions are critical to success (or failure). For small
retailers, which have only a few locations, each decision has the potential to make or break the company.

As a result, it is important for the modern retail manager to be familiar with the process of choosing a location and store format. It is equally
important for retailers to establish systems to evaluate past real estate
decisions. Putting aside unique locations intended to build the brand

rather than the bottom line, we can assess retail store performance by a few key metrics.

If location is about convenience for the customer, then location and format decisions are about making consumption as convenient as possible for the right consumers. Of course, distribution routes, distance to warehouses, cannibalization, competition, and other logistical concerns also matter; but if a retailer does not attract enough of the right customers, those other concerns are trivial. To put it another way: those other concerns are about profitability, but first and foremost, location is about revenue – that is, getting the right customers to spend at your store and not those of your competitors. Without revenue, there is no profit.

When evaluating a store location or comparing several locations, it is often helpful to break revenue and profitability down by square footage. This allows retailers to compare different store sizes, formats, and locations within a chain. Retailers also use these metrics to compare themselves to the competition. The calculation simply takes the total revenue (or profit) and divides by the square footage of the store. This metric is usually stated in annual terms and can vary greatly between different types of retailers. As a general benchmark, many retailers consider $400 to $500 in annual sales per square foot to be a reasonable level of productivity. At the high end, retailers such as Tiffany and Co. and the Apple Store can produce five or ten times that number. Although annual per square foot measures are very broad and provide only a high-level overview of store activity, they are a central metric for evaluating retail performance. The year-over-year comparison within the same store is especially important in evaluating retail success. Retail growth can come through mergers and acquisitions; however, analysts and investors tend to prefer growth driven by existing stores that improve their performance relative to the previous year on a per square foot basis.

Another key measure for evaluating a retail location is its ability to generate traffic and convert that traffic into sales. Traffic is simply a count of how many people enter the store. Conversion is calculated by dividing the number of people who purchase by the total traffic count. In its simplest form, conversion involves the retailer in manually recording how many people enter the store and using the number of sales receipts as the numerator to calculate conversion. More sophisticated approaches – often implemented by third-party companies – can automate the conversion calculation by integrating an electronic count of the number of people who come through the store with point-of-sale (POS) systems.

The absolute level of traffic and conversion may be informative, but ultimately retailers are interested in the trends over time between different stores in the chain and relative to the competition. Although these metrics are only rough measures of how effectively a store attracts customers and makes sales, they can provide valuable insight into retail performance. Holding constant other factors – such as sales promotions and years in operation – when one store in a chain struggles to generate sufficient traffic, it can signal a poor location decision. When conversion figures are lower than expected, retailers tend to look at their in-store performance. This can range from reconsidering the store's layout and internal signage to additional training for the sales staff to making the checkout process faster. Too much traffic can result in lower conversion numbers – possibly because sales staff cannot spend as much time with each consumer who enters the store – even when the store generates reasonable sales per square foot. In combination, these metrics provide a good set of baseline measures for evaluating the performance of a retail store.

Chapter Four

Inside the Store

In 1916, Clarence Saunders opened Piggly Wiggly, the first self-service grocery store, in Memphis, Tennessee, and changed the world of retailing. Prior to 1916, almost all shopping for basic and staple goods was done at local "full service" general merchandise stores. The full-service approach meant a shopper would tell a store clerk what items he or she wished to purchase and the clerk would collect them. The shopper would receive the items in the store or have them home delivered, and the cost of the purchases was added to his or her credit account. This process was expensive for retailers. First, the personal care provided to each shopper, and the compilation of items for delivery, took a great deal of staff time and attention. Second, selling predominantly on credit meant retailers had to carry the costs of their inventory beyond the sale, which increased the risk that full payment for the purchased items would be substantially delayed or even defaulted.

To address these issues, Saunders introduced the first self-service grocery store, which required that customers choose their own items, put them in a basket, and take them to a checkout counter. In addition, Piggly Wiggly adopted a cash-and-carry approach that required customers to pay in cash and in full at the time they purchased their groceries. As a result, Saunders could sell more items to more people in less time and with fewer staff. This allowed Piggly Wiggly to buy inventory in larger quantities and negotiate lower prices. Although initially there were many skeptics, the response from customers was positive, and over the next six years Saunders grew the chain to 659 corporate-owned stores and 582 franchise stores across forty-one states and into Canada.[1] To facilitate such rapid expansion, Saunders built on his initial ideas for a self-service grocery store and pioneered several other innovations that have since become standard retail practices. He is credited with being the first to provide checkout stands, attach a sticker price to every individual item in the store, use refrigerated cases to keep produce fresher longer, and put employees in uniforms that aimed to improve sanitary food handling.[2] Competitors quickly adopted similar strategies.

Consumers strongly preferred this type of store, which was convenient and offered lower prices. Retailers moved away from serving customers directly and began to focus on offering products for sale. They became increasingly passive merchants – they stocked merchandise on shelves and waited at the exits to collect payment. Today, many retailers continue to push the boundaries by including in-aisle price checking stations, in-store product information kiosks, and self-checkouts. Human resources are one of the three big costs retailers face – along with inventory and real estate – and so the greater the extent to which customers can serve themselves, the more money retailers save. Today, for better or worse, a customer can complete an entire in-store shopping trip without ever interacting with an employee.

In-Store Shopper Marketing

At a general level, consumers' purchase decisions fall into one of three categories. First, there are those they make before they enter the store. For example, they might have a shopping list that includes specific items – such as "no pulp" Tropicana orange juice in a 1.9-liter container, relaxed-fit jeans from Gap with a thirty-inch waist and thirty-two-inch inseam, or a size six pink Nike hoodie. Upon entering the store, customers navigate directly to the shelf containing the product they want to purchase.

The second type of purchase is planned at the general category level – for example, orange juice or jeans or a child's hoodie. With a general plan, customers head to the section of the store – or the store within a shopping center – that offers those particular products for sale. They then choose from among the available products. The third type of purchase is unplanned. For example, while traveling toward the orange juice, customers might pass by the bakery and spontaneously decide to purchase a loaf of freshly baked French bread. Similarly, they might be waiting in line to pay for the planned Nike hoodie when their daughter convinces them she also needs a new headband. A store employee can also generate unplanned purchases by recommending a top to go with new jeans.

As it turns out, these unplanned purchases are critical to retail success. As Underhill says, "If we went into stores only when we needed to buy something, and if once there we bought only what we needed, the economy would collapse, boom."[3] From a retailer's perspective, this means that what happens once the consumer gets into a store drives a substantial share of that store's revenue. Put another way, the in-store environment is a critical component of the retail value proposition.

Managing the Probability of Purchase

To better understand how the in-store environment affects consumer decisions, it is helpful to think in terms of the probability of the three general categories of purchasing. In other words, on a particular shopping trip, what is the probability that a consumer will make (1) an unplanned purchase, (2) a generally planned purchase, or (3) a specifically planned purchase, and what factors within the store environment influence these probabilities?

Recent research has begun to answer these questions. In a particularly insightful project, Jeff Inman, Russell Winer, and Rosellina Ferraro examine data from the grocery industry. The data, collected by the Point of Purchase Advertising Institute (POPAI), included in-store intercept interviews with 2,300 consumers at twenty-eight grocery stores across fourteen geographically dispersed cities in the United States.[4] The results clearly demonstrate the critical importance of in-store factors on consumer decision.

First, the authors find that after controlling for the personal characteristics of individual customers (e.g., gender, household size, store familiarity, etc.) and the nature of the product category (e.g., type of products, coupon use, in-store displays, etc.), the baseline probability of an unplanned purchase was 0.46. That is, the likelihood that an individual consumer will make an unplanned purchase on a given shopping trip is 46 percent. However, they also find that the probability of an unplanned purchase could increase to as high as 93 percent depending on the shopping context.

Time for Coffee

One of the most important determinants of the probability of purchase is the time spent shopping. Inman, Winer, and Ferraro find that the longer customers were in the store the more likely they were to make an unplanned purchase.[5] This is consistent with what other retail market researchers have discovered in their observations of in-store consumer behavior and is not particularly novel news for most retail managers. However, some retailers are more successful than others at implementing changes to their store environment to encourage longer shopping trips.

Grocers, for example, has simultaneously slowed and enhanced the shopping experience by putting cafés and coffee kiosks into their stores. In doing so, they have found that customers are less rushed, more relaxed, and more likely to enjoy grocery shopping. As a result, customers who buy a coffee tend to stay in the store for a longer period and spend more money.

Shopper Efficiency: Seconds per Dollar

At the same time, research and common sense dictate that just spending more time in a store is not necessarily going to drive sales. What matters is what the customer does with that time. In the grocery store example, the customer who buys a coffee during a shopping trip slows down and spends more money. However, the grocer could also have increased the time spent in its stores by reducing the number of open cash registers. Fewer cash registers would have created longer line-ups, which would have ensured that most customers – other than those who abandon their carts and leave – would spend more time in the store. However, time spent waiting is not productive time; in fact, the longer people wait in line, the less satisfied they tend to be with the overall shopping experience. Increasing the time consumers spend in line is unlikely to increase the amount they spend on their current shopping trip, and is likely to reduce the probability that they will return for future trips.

Herb Sorensen, founder of ShopperScientist LLC and author of *Inside the Mind of the Shopper*, argues that retailers need to focus on increasing shoppers' efficiency. Specifically, he says that retailers should minimize the time it takes a shopper to spend a dollar. Sorensen believes that seconds (spent in-store) per dollar of sales is the most important metric in retailing. Essentially, he contends that retailers should focus on connecting consumers with the products they want to buy as efficiently as possible, even if the consumer did not plan to buy those products before entering the store. In other words, retailers want customers to spend more time in their stores, and they want that time to be spent efficiently – that is, both maximizing the total time spent in the store and minimizing the seconds spent in store per dollar of sales generated. This is a balancing act. For some McDonald's locations, efficiency might mean bright lighting, plastic seats, and meal combos that encourage an accelerated dining experience. For other McDonald's locations, it might mean fireplaces, more comfortable seating, and less intense lighting.

Making Shopping ESE

To a large extent, discussions about store locations, formats, and in-store designs are really about making the shopping experience *convenient* for consumers. In a world where many consumers are time-starved, an easier and more convenient shopping experience is a more valuable one. Convenience is not as simple as proximity. Instead, it comes from ESE – that is, how the retailer designs the environment, selection, and engagement components of the retail value proposition affects how convenient the experience feels to the consumer. These components are not independent of each other.

While the average big-box store carries between 30,000 and 50,000 products, the average consumer household buys only 300 distinct items per year. This means that the average consumer will not purchase more than 99 percent of the products a big-box retailer has in stock.[6] That is not to say that 99 percent of the products are never purchased – each household buys a different set of 300 items each year – but it does mean that the average customer has to navigate through tens of thousands of available items to find the few she wants to purchase on any particular shopping trip.

As Barry Schwarz documents in *The Paradox of Choice*, too much choice is overwhelming for many people and results in consumers who are less satisfied with the shopping experience, which ultimately hurts retail profitability. Consider, for example, a consumer who wants a product to relieve her cold symptoms. First, she has to decide where to shop for such a product. Over-the-counter pharmaceuticals are now commonly available in a variety of locations ranging from hotel gift shops and convenience stores to drug and grocery stores. Once she has chosen a store and is standing in front of the shelf, the consumer faces a dizzying array of products from a variety of brands with a broad spectrum of ingredients. Even within a particular brand, she can choose products that vary in when they should be taken (day, night, every four hours, every eight hours, etc.), how they can be taken (caplet, gel cap, tablet, with food, without food, etc.), and what symptoms they treat (headache, fever, congestion, body aches, etc.). She must also decide whether to buy a brand name product or a generic product with the same or similar active ingredients. Each version comes with a different price and a different number of pills in the package. Ironically, all this choice is enough to make a healthy person ill.

To effectively address the burden of too much choice, and to make shopping easier and more efficient for a growing segment of time-starved shoppers, retailers have become increasingly focused on improving their in-store designs and thereby increasing the probability of purchase.

Knowing You Have Arrived

The entrance or *transition zone* is one of the most critical and underappreciated areas of retail. The first few steps a customer takes into a store set the stage for the shopping experience; yet, many retailers have narrow entrances with multiple doors and lined with product displays. As I mentioned earlier, sales and profitability per square foot are important retail metrics and, as a result, many merchants want to minimize non-productive store space. In general, this makes sense. Retailers are in the business of selling products and should use floor space to optimize the display of those products. However, retailers should also design the entrance to a store as the gateway to the consumer experience.

If a store's retail value proposition is built around selection, then the first few steps into the store should signal that selection. Electronics stores, such as Best Buy, have been known do this with a wall of TVs, visible from the first step into the store. Grocery stores often begin the shopping experience in the retailer's showpiece produce section. Some drugstores open with the cosmetics section, which can be an important point of differentiation for pharmacy chains. Unfortunately, rather than using the first few steps inside the store to say "welcome" – or better yet, "welcome back" – too many retailers jump right into "buy this." Ironically, the former approach makes customers feel like buying, while the latter puts them on alert and triggers a defensive mindset.

Once customers make the transition into the store, they begin to move about. In many cases, that means heading to the right and moving in a roughly counter-clockwise manner.[7] Of course, this is not always the case, and where a customer goes depends on several factors, such as how familiar she is with the store, where her desired products are located, where other shoppers are going, how the aisles are arranged, what attracts her attention, and so on. Some customers are on a mission: they know exactly what they want and where to find it. They are not there to browse but are focused on getting in and getting out. Stores that cater to such customers make the shopping experience as efficient as possible. However, research suggests that shoppers are 13 percent more likely to make an unplanned purchase when they visit most aisles in a store and 24 percent more likely to make an unplanned purchase when they visit every aisle.[8] Once again, retailers need to know what type of customer they serve and design their store interiors accordingly.

The Land of Aisles

Over time, retailers have learned that some product categories are best displayed up front and others are best displayed deeper into the store. Grocery stores, for example, tend to put milk at the back of the store and chocolate bars at the cash register because one product is a staple and the other is a more discretionary impulse purchase. The average grocery shopper is much more likely to have milk on the list than a chocolate bar, but when she is waiting in line to pay, the presence of the chocolate bar increases the probability of an unplanned purchase. Sporting goods stores tend put services such as bike repair and skate sharpening in locations that introduce customers to new products and encourage browsing during the wait. Liquor stores put cold beer at the back, and drugstores do the same with pharmacies. This is not happenstance – it is a deliberate attempt to use destination products to expose customers to more of the store. But this is only the beginning.

THE GRID LAYOUT

Retailers have several generic store layouts on which to base their interiors. The most common approach is the grid, in which aisles are organized parallel to each other with shelves on both sides. This layout is popular because it is efficient. Customers are familiar with this type of store, are comfortable moving around in it, and can quickly find the products they want to buy. It is also cost-efficient for the retailer, because the interior fixtures can be standardized, and a great deal of merchandise can be displayed per square foot. Larger grocery and warehouse stores, with tens of thousands of products, emphasize efficiency and, as a result, favor the grid layout. In exchange for efficiency, however, the grid format makes it more difficult for the retailer to influence the flow of shopper traffic. To address this limitation, stores have become very creative with their signage and product displays (more on this below).

In supercenters, which can exceed 100,000 square feet, even the grid layout can be difficult to navigate. As a result, managers at these hypermarkets find themselves rescuing customers who have become seriously lost within the store. With an aging population, mobility is another issue of increasing concern, and stores have found a growing segment of the population appreciates being able to borrow a scooter to drive up and down wide aisles rather than trying to navigate on foot.

RACETRACKS AND RECTANGLES

The racetrack is an alternative generic store layout. This style of store design is common in large apparel and department stores, features an extra-wide aisle that loops around the periphery of the store, and, in theory, guides the customer from department to department. Shelving within each department can include a grid design, but often also incorporates low-lying tables, racks at different angles, and category-specific displays to attract shoppers and encourage them to browse the merchandise.

Smaller stores tend to use a less structured layout, which includes shelving that lines the interior walls along with a variety of displays through the middle of the store. This type of design is typical of a mall or street-level store smaller than 5,000 square feet. Usually these stores are rectangular in shape, which allows the retailer to create many different types of interior traffic patterns.

Traffic Flow

In practice, most successful retailers have modified these generic store designs to reflect the type of traffic flow they want to create, as well as the specific needs of the customer segments they want to target. The Apple Store, for example, tends to use a basic rectangular unstructured approach. However, Apple Stores also minimize the number of products on display – which typically include only a few different models of each device – and encourage customers to touch and try the floor models. In addition, Apple Stores use a mobile payment process that means customers do not have to find a cash register, but just need a salesperson with a handheld device.

IKEA is well known for its innovative in-store design that funnels shoppers along a winding path through various departments and product displays. This approach ensures that most customers see a full range of products, including those they do not immediately plan to buy. This can be frustrating for the customer who just wants to pick up a pillow but is an effective approach that differentiates IKEA's shopping experience and encourages customers to spend more time in the store. With a nod toward shopping efficiency, the retailer also includes a few "short cuts" that allow customers to escape the full tour.

What They See Is What They Get

Ultimately, the interior design and layout of a retail store is a balancing act between customer convenience and product exposure. Academic research and decades of retail experience clearly demonstrate that a store's design and layout can impact the probability of purchase. Retailers have been intensely interested in optimizing their interior designs since customers were first allowed to roam free and select products for themselves.

However, studies indicate that, in general, retailers are surprisingly poor at creating environments that meet their customers' needs when it comes to efficiently finding and evaluating in-store products. For example, in a large survey, Raymond Burke discovered that American customers are generally satisfied with product quality and pricing – that is, the aspects of retailing that have received the most attention in recent years.[9]

In contrast, customers are most dissatisfied with the level of the service they receive, their ability to find information about the available products, and the speed with which they can complete their shopping tasks. Enhanced in-store marketing can address these problems, beginning with a better understanding of aisle and shelf *value zones*.

Aisle Value Zones

Not all areas of a retail store are equally valuable. In fact, many retailers find that when they map their sales onto a store's interior layout, a small percentage of the floor space accounts for a large percentage of the overall sales. This might be the bestsellers' shelf at Barnes and Noble, the women's sweatshirts and yoga pants displays at lululemon, the pharmacy at Walgreen's drug stores, and so on.

However, beyond the destination product categories and the natural flow in and out of the store, research indicates that shoppers are significantly less likely to visit products shelved further into an aisle and substantially more likely to notice and consider buying products shelved closer to the end of an aisle.[10] The average consumer is a *boomerang shopper* – that is, she tends to navigate retail stores by moving around the perimeter and darting into an aisle or section only as far as she needs to go to find what she wants.[11]

Once consumers locate the target product in an aisle, they tend to turn back to the perimeter rather than continuing forward. During this trip, most people look directly at where they are going until they reach their destination. This means they only see products in their peripheral vision as they look for their target product. As consumers near the products they are interested in, they tend to turn and face the shelf. After making a decision to buy the product (or not), they head straight back out of the aisle. Other than the section that displays the target products, consumers tend to see very little beyond the ends of the aisle.

END CAPS

Retailers emphasize the end caps of aisles because they tend to get more attention, even among mission-driven shoppers. Attention does not guarantee a sale, but if customers fail to see the product in the store, they will not buy it. Other specialized product displays positioned in key, often high-traffic, locations throughout a store can help to convert browsers to buyers and increase the average amount consumers spend. For example, Inman and colleagues found that in-store product displays increase the probability of an unplanned purchase by 39 percent.[12] End caps work well because they take advantage of the traffic that flows past them as consumers move around the perimeter of the store and dart in and out of aisles. Retailers, however, can be more active in their influence over customers' shopping paths.

OPEN SPACES

Consumers like personal space, and tend to be repelled by overcrowded store sections and drawn toward more comfortable environments. This can include open areas within a store, wider aisles, or even shelving that allows for less obstructed views of the products and the rest of the store. For example, table-level displays and other types of shelving people can see over tend to create a greater sense of space. Similarly, pyramid-shaped shelves can give shoppers the illusion of being less closed in.[13]

Open space and aisle width also have practical implications for important consumer segments. For example, wider aisles are imperative when aiming to attract the valuable mothers-with-young-children consumer segment. If a stroller loaded up with a couple of kids and a days' worth of supplies does not fit down an aisle or through a section, then time-starved and convenience-driven mothers are not likely to go there. Similarly, as the population ages, seniors increasingly shop with mobility constraints. When stores do not have wide aisles and open spaces, they are very inconvenient for shoppers who use walkers and wheelchairs.

ACTIVITY ZONES

Activity zones are akin to open spaces. These areas influence traffic patterns by drawing a large volume of shoppers from across the store. There are many examples of such zones in both large and small retail environments. Williams-Sonoma has sampling stations and cooking displays; REI includes a climbing wall; Disney Stores have magic mirrors and car repair centers; Teavana provides a "smelling bar" with samples of the scents of dozens of teas; and the Microsoft store has gaming areas. In addition to influencing the flow of traffic, these areas contribute substantially to the feel and experience of shopping in the store. Although the grandiose interiors of a Marshall Field's or Harrods are rare, even modern utilitarian store designs can increase their appeal by creating activity zones that enhance shoppers' experience beyond extracting dollars from wallets.

LIGHTING AND ATMOSPHERICS

Lighting is another way to attract attention and draw customers toward a product. For example, grocery stores will use lighting to focus on produce displays. This approach draws shoppers' attention to the produce and makes it easy to navigate from one section to another. Trendy apparel stores from Abercrombie & Fitch to Hugo Boss use lighting to call customers' attention to particular displays or areas of the store. In addition to directing attention, atmospherics such as lighting can influence consumers' moods. Natural lighting, for example, has been shown to decrease negative feelings among consumers and increase both the average amount they spend and their willingness to pay.[14]

In fact, using interior design elements – including lighting, color, scent, and music[15] – to make customers feel better has the potential to substantially improve the shopping experience and increase consumer spending. For example, in a study of two IKEA stores with different atmospheres (i.e., layout, interior colors, recent renovations, furniture presentation, etc.), German researcher Kordelia Spies and colleagues found that how pleasant consumers perceived a store's interior to be dramatically affected their behavior.[16] In particular, stores with more pleasant environments stimulated positive feelings in their customers. More importantly, Spies's results demonstrate that when a store's interior makes customers feel better, they spend more money. As a science, retail atmospherics is still in its infancy, and in the years to come there is likely to be a great deal of innovation in this area as interior designers begin to work with market researchers to build more customer-centric sensory shopping environments.

SIGNAGE

Signs are one of the oldest methods to capture attention and direct customers within a store. In-store signs remain an important influence on consumer behavior. However, observational research indicates that how effective a sign is can really only be assessed within the store environment. Retail stores are visually busy, potentially overwhelming, very dynamic environments that resist attempts to generalize about what works best. Underhill argues that his marketing research and consulting firm needs to "watch shopper after shopper for hours on end, hundreds of people, thousands of minutes, and then assemble our findings before we can say whether a sign is any good."[17] If that is true, most retailers will not invest in measuring the effectiveness of the many, many signs they have throughout their stores – on a sign-by-sign basis, the return on investment is unlikely to justify the effort. The exception is large retail chains undergoing major renovations that include standardizing signage across many different stores.

What we do know is a very general set of guidelines: less is more, bigger is better, and lower prices are preferred. "Less is more" because retail environments are naturally visually demanding. From interior designs down to individual product packages, merchants and manufacturers fight for consumers' attention. As a result, the fewer signs a retailer uses in a particular area of the store, the more likely it is that customers will notice each sign and process the information it displays. "Bigger is better" refers to the size of the typeface on the sign. People do not like fine print and mistrust signs that read like legal contracts. Large and clear typefaces are easy to see and efficient to process.

I talk more about pricing in chapter 11, but at this point it is worth acknowledging the obvious: all else being equal, consumers prefer lower prices. Strategically, competing on price alone is not sustainable for most retailers. Nevertheless, there are times when in-store promotions can help move products that are not selling as well as the retailer would like or can create excitement that draws customers to the store and keeps them looking around a little longer. Research suggests that in-store coupons can be especially useful in this regard. Specifically, coupons that hang directly in front of the product on the shelf have been shown, on average, to increase sales by 35 percent and enhance profitability by more than 100 percent.[18]

Simple directional signs can have an important impact on the customer experience. Even signs that highlight the bathrooms and checkout counters can be helpful. Customers do not like to wait in line, but if they must, they like to know where they are supposed to stand. Surprisingly, many retailers provide customers with little consistent guidance on where to pay and where to wait, an oversight that can ruin an otherwise pleasant shopping experience.

DENSITY AND FREQUENCY

To better understand where customers go and what they look at, many retailers and industry consultants use heat, density, and frequency maps that aggregate consumers' traffic patterns to highlight areas that draw and hold the most shoppers. In some cases, this is done through observation, either in person or using in-store cameras. However, more sophisticated techniques are increasingly common. For example, researchers at the Wharton School at the University of Pennsylvania have used radio-frequency identification (RFID) tags embedded in shopping carts to track customers' movements around grocery stores.[19] In the years to come, cameras with facial recognition, loyalty cards with embedded RFID chips, as well as apps that use global positioning systems (GPS) and wireless tracking on mobile devices may serve a similar purpose.

Shelf Value Zones

From the consumer's perspective, the point of navigating through a store is to find products to evaluate and potentially purchase. Ultimately, this goal brings consumers to a shelf or product display.

Merchants have long known that customers do not buy what they do not see. More recently, retailers and product manufacturers have realized that a large portion of the consumer decision-making process happens at the shelf, facing the products. To convert more customers and increase their average "spend," retailers increasingly focus on managing product displays.

The basic shelf space management tool for most retailers is the "planogram" or "modular" that lays out how products should be displayed and positioned on the shelf. Some companies use very simple, even hand-drawn, illustrations that provide a rough guideline for what goes where. Others use pictures of what the shelf should look like based on plans designed by the visual merchandising team. In a growing number of cases, retailers are introducing sophisticated software that is connected to both supply chain and customer information systems. Regardless of how they are developed, plan-o-grams can be useful tools for standardizing shelf space and design.

STOOP AND STRETCH

The shelf value zone hierarchy is the key principle underlying the design of a plan-o-gram. Similar to aisles, shelves can be divided into different areas of effectiveness. The bottom 24 inches of a shelf are known as the "stoop zone," and this zone's display value is relatively low, simply because products at that level are often overlooked. In addition, consumers do not like to bend over – and risk a "butt brush" – to view products in the stoop zone. Shelf space above 70 inches is in the "stretch zone," which generally has the lowest display value because the products there are difficult to see or reach without assistance. Products in the stretch and stoop zones, in most cases, sell relatively poorly. As a result, many retailers either do not shelve products in these zones, or use them for product storage rather than display.

SIGHT AND GRAB

The high-value zones are right in front of the consumer's eyes and hands. The "sight zone" is the highest value section of the shelf, normally considered to be at a height of between 55 and 70 inches. When consumers face the shelf, they cannot help but see products in this zone. In addition, products at this level are more likely to be seen in consumers' peripheral vision as they walk past the shelf. The next most valuable space is the "grab zone" at about 24 to 55 inches. This zone is not directly in the line of sight for most consumers; however, it is easy to see and very easy to touch products at this level. In cases where touch might be even more important than sight – for example, with some food and apparel products – this can be a very valuable product position.

KIDS AND PETS

Of course, retailers need to use common sense in the application of these general principles to their own store designs. For example, the value zones are different in children's toy stores and pet stores. Kids and pets have much lower sight and grab zones, and are happy to interact with products right down to the floor level. In such cases, shelf sections over 48 inches may become stretch zones and have value only insofar as they keep products away from kids and pets and aim instead at the parent and owner segment.

Packaging

When you think of some brands – such as Tide, Coca-Cola, Method, Absolut Vodka, and DeWalt – it is likely that their consistent package designs come to mind. Products like these have built their brands on the ease with which they are recognized. They pop out in advertisements, on in-store signage, and on the shelf because they are deeply ingrained in many consumers' minds. As a result, packaging is a critical part of a product's ability to break through the clutter in advertisements outside the store and on the shelf inside the store. When product lines from Method and DeWalt were first launched, a great deal of time and attention went into creating a look and feel that appealed to a target consumer segment, grabbed attention, and rapidly built recognition. For a customer looking at a tool shelf, DeWalt's consistent use of yellow and black stands out against otherwise strong competing brands.

For consumer segments looking for product information as a part of their evaluation process, it is important to ensure that packaging clearly communicates the key benefits of the product over those of the competition. Much like signage, less is more, bigger is better, and lower prices are preferred. In addition, some consumers prefer products with packages that make them easier to use post-purchase. A classic example in this regard is food packaged for consumption "on-the-go" or products like ketchup in "easy squeeze" or "fridge-door fit" containers. In highly competitive product categories, these little differences can turn into a big advantage.

The Importance of the End

After consumers navigate the store and select the products they want to purchase, their experience concludes in the cash-wrap area. A poor payment process can ruin a great shopping experience, and a great cash-wrap experience can save a poor shopping experience. Inattentive, bored, or rude checkout staff can have a disastrous effect on an otherwise beautifully designed and expertly executed in-store environment. Even if the staff are phenomenal, not all customers are. These "demon" customers tend to be unprofitable because of the time and attention they demand, but they can also upset employees and ruin the experience for other shoppers (see chapter 9). Overall, from the retailer's perspective, the end of the experience is a risky point of consumer contact.

To improve the checkout experience, many retailers find it helpful to deal with returns and complaints at a specialized counter away from the cash-wrap area. As a result, the customers who enjoyed shopping at the store and are satisfied with their purchase do not have to wait in line behind a dissatisfied customer and hear about their problems with the store and its products. Retailers can also ease frustration by minimizing checkout delays. For example, Lowe's has aggressively promoted its policy of opening another register whenever there is a line of more than three customers.

Although minimizing delays is not always possible or profitable, most retailers can implement tactics that reduce the pain of waiting. However, this requires a different perspective on the cash-wrap area. Many retailers design their checkout process as if the shopping experience is over and the payment experience has started. Instead, the cash-wrap area is space in which to encourage unplanned purchases, educate customers for future purchases, entertain, and make a positive last – and hopefully lasting – impression.

During most of a typical shopping trip, consumers move rapidly, focus on where they are going, and ignore most of what the retailer is offering. However, when they stand in line, they become a captive audience. This is a unique opportunity for the retailer. A well-designed cash-wrap area can generate incremental sales, whether of a pack of batteries or chewing gum. The challenge for retailers is to balance the opportunity to display items with the potential negative effects of the wrong items or too many items. For example, while chocolate bars and candy are a positive impulse purchase for many adults, parents dread spending time in line pulling these treats from their children's hands.

While wrestling with a toddler can make a couple of minutes in line feel like hours, other aspects of the checkout experience can make time pass more quickly. For example, although most grocery shoppers do not buy the tabloids displayed in the cash-wrap area, they can derive entertainment from perusing the headlines about celebrity drama. Similarly, some retailers have introduced video screens at the check-out, either as part of the cash register or as a separate display. Video screens can distract customers from the time they spend in line as they watch entertaining and educational clips that range from upcoming promotions and product demonstrations to the retailer's involvement in local charities.

What Customers Want

With all of these tools at the retailer's disposal, you might think that consumers are simply being led from display to display looking at what retailers want them to look at and buying what retailers want them to buy. In fact, nothing could be farther from the truth. Today's shoppers are sophisticated decision makers and increasingly have the means to quickly and easily grab product information – and even competitors' prices – off their mobile devices while they shop.

Aisle and shelf space management is about making it convenient for consumers to find what they want and easy for them to buy what they find. Retailers who aim to trick or manipulate customers risk trading a transaction today for a customer for life. For example, the work of Inman, Winer, and Ferraro suggests that people who shop with a list – just over 50 percent of all customers – are about 10 percent less likely to make an unplanned purchase.[20] But that does not make the list the enemy of the retailer. List shoppers are also likely to be more efficient shoppers who spend more dollars per second in the store. It would be foolish for a retailer to focus its efforts on turning a consumer who is picking up milk and a loaf of bread into a two-hundred-dollar shopping cart.

Similarly, Inman, Winer, and Ferraro's research finds that customers who use out-of-store coupons are about 30 percent less likely to make an unplanned purchase. That does not mean retailers should eliminate coupons, but it should raise a red flag for those that want to increase the average amount spent by customers. Coupons are about price discrimination. A small number of customers are willing to put in the time and effort to clip coupons related to the products they plan to purchase and bring those coupons to the store to save money. Coupons are an effective way to attract and retain that price-sensitive segment. However, companies that use coupons as an advertising tool may want to carefully monitor the impact on their business over the long term. As I discuss in chapter 9, not every customer is good for business.

Measuring Success

In this chapter, I have talked about applying the basics of in-store design and shopper marketing to create an environment that contributes to a compelling retail value proposition. The key metrics from previous chapters are still critically important here – including the continued focus on revenue and profit. However, I have also introduced the importance of engaging customers and understanding the flow of traffic through a store. To successfully manage traffic flow, a retailer needs to know where customers shop and how they move around. As I discussed earlier, this can be done through traffic density and frequency maps based on either observation or emerging technological solutions.

The time a customer spends in the store is also a critical measure. However, it is a measure that has to be interpreted within the retailer's overall strategic position. For some stores and some consumer segments, it makes sense to focus on efficiency – that is, how much money customers spend per unit of time (e.g., dollars per second). Retailers that take this approach emphasize convenience and ease of shopping as they design their store environments. Other companies focus on maximizing the time consumers spend in the store. These retailers focus on a pleasant shopping experience that encourages greater exploration of the aisles, shelves, and products.

Other metrics that are relevant to assessing the in-store environment address how customers move, where they go, whether or not they buy, and how much they spend. To better understand their own customer base, retailers may want to measure the boomerang rate – that is, what percentage of consumers pop in and out of an aisle (versus completing the entire aisle). This can be further broken down into how far they go into each aisle. Similarly, many retailers want to understand how many customers shop for a particular item or small set of items at an accelerated pace. Both the mission and the boomerang rate can be even more valuable when examined in terms of customer segments and segmentation variables (demographic, geographic, psychographic, and behavioral).

When evaluating the in-store environment, retailers should attend to the average time spent in the store per customer; the traffic in the store during different times, days, and seasons; and the conversion rate (i.e., what percentage of the traffic makes a purchase). Finally, because real estate is one of the big three costs in retailing along with employees and inventory, it is important for retailers to look at their sales and profitability in terms of sales per square foot and profit per square foot. However, given that different aisles and shelf zones have different values, some retailers may want to push this further to understand their sales and profits in specific areas throughout the store.

Chapter Five

Omnichannel Retailing

Store location, design, and format decisions define the shopping environment because the majority of purchase decisions still happen within the walls of a bricks and mortar retail outlet. Nevertheless, ever since Montgomery Ward and Sears Roebuck built thriving catalog businesses more than a century ago, retailers have known that customers like to have multiple ways to buy. In response, enterprising businesses have experimented with several alternative sales channels that have included everything from catalogs and home shopping television to door-to-door sales and hosted in-home parties. Although such approaches have found some success among niche segments, their overall impact on retailing has been limited.

In contrast, the impact of electronic retailing has been dramatic. The 1990s ushered in the era of online shopping with fanfare and hyperbole. Companies with few customers and little or no business plan attracted billions of investment dollars. Consumers were promised unprecedented access to products at extremely low prices. Retailers were told they could sell to more people with minimal investments in staff and real estate. Pundits predicted the death of traditional retailers and retail formats.

Then the dot-com bubble burst, and sentiment swung almost as wildly in the other direction. Online retailers failed as quickly as they had appeared – some in spectacular fashion – while many traditional retailers substantially reduced investment in new media or even eliminated their e-commerce presence. However, throughout the dramatic ups and downs, a growing number of consumers began to incorporate online shopping and information search into their buying behavior. Although Internet and other electronic sales channels (TV, mobile, etc.) continue to represent only a small share of total retail revenue, online and mobile revenue is growing at a rate that is an order of magnitude greater than in-store sales. While many retailers struggle to achieve year-over-year sales growth of 2 to 3 percent, online sales have increased by more than 25 percent per year.[1] As a result, one of the most pressing questions retailers face is how to develop and manage their sales across a diverse and seemingly ever-growing variety of sales channels to generate a solid return on investment. Unfortunately, rapid changes in technology, as well as constant innovations in e-commerce and communications, have made the development of robust and reliable tactics for managing electronic retailing extremely challenging. Nevertheless, in the modern marketplace, a retail value proposition needs to consider both the physical and electronic environments that the target customers shop in. "Omnichannel retailing" is a term that has been coined to capture the shift in consumer behavior from traditional shopping across multiple channels – such as physical stores, websites, catalogs, and so on – to an overall shopping experience that breaks down distinctions between physical and electronic shopping. An omnichannel retailer focuses on the consumer experience that augments reality to turn the world into a showroom and to make the buying process possible from anywhere at any time.

The Rapid Evolution of Omnichannel Retailing

In 1995, only 14 percent of Americans used the Internet.[2] A decade later, 66 percent used the Internet,[3] and today just under 90 percent of American households have a broadband Internet connection.[4]

As Internet access expanded, consumers began to change the way they bought products in a variety of categories. Amazon led the way by redefining retailing for books and CDs. Computer companies such as Dell took advantage of the new ease with which they could directly connect to consumers and demonstrated the power of a business model that allowed customers to participate in the design of the products they purchased. Similarly, travelers were quick to adopt self-service websites that offered then-unprecedented convenience and control. The entertainment industry underwent dramatic changes and was forced to revolutionize the distribution of music, movies, and television. Initially, consumers migrated to gray-market websites, such as Napster, which allowed users to share files for free with their peers. Later, companies such as Apple and Netflix led the development of more structured channels for the distribution of electronic content.

Categories ranging from automobiles and residential real estate to furniture and appliances have struggled to deal with better-informed consumers who know what they want to buy and how much they should pay. The Yellow Pages, which not so long ago was an indispensable part of advertising and promotion for many retailers, has been replaced by web pages that offer more information in a more convenient format. Traditional forms of advertising – from print to radio to television – continue to be under siege as marketers move large portions of their promotional budgets into electronic media channels. Google's AdWords, in particular, has changed the way many retailers reach their customers. Beyond the Internet, retailers today have to consider the ability of customers to check product reviews and competitors' prices on their mobile devices while they shop in-store.

Facebook quickly became a powerful influence on consumer behavior because it facilitated consumer-to-consumer word-of-mouth communication. Facebook was not open to the public until the fall of 2006, yet the company had more than 1.4 billion monthly active users at the end of March 2015,[5] and about half of all Americans use the social networking site at least once per month.[6] At the same time, older social networking sites like MySpace have steadily lost users. Bebo, a social networking pioneer, which looked very promising when AOL purchased it in the spring of 2008 for $850 million, failed to gain critical mass, went bankrupt in 2013, was bought by its original founders for $1 million, and is now back as a messaging app.[7] Twitter grew rapidly from its launch in 2006 to more than 302 million active users in 2015, who produce more than 500 million 140-character tweets per day.

More recently, the rise of online couponing services, such as Groupon and LivingSocial, has directly affected retail pricing.[8] Groupon, for example, was launched in November 2008 to offer daily deals on a wide variety of consumer purchases ranging from restaurants to hair salons to clothing. It promptly expanded to more than 300 markets in more than thirty-five countries and soon became one of the fastest companies in history to grow to $1 billion in annual revenue.[9] In October 2010, Yahoo! offered to buy Groupon for $3 billion, and in November 2010, Google offered to pay $6 billion. Groupon turned both companies down, and its initial public offering in November 2011 was valued at almost $13 billion – the largest IPO by a U.S. Internet company since Google.[10] The fall of Groupon was equally stunning. By 2013, the CEO and one of the company's founders, Andrew Mason, was fired, and the stock price was down 75 percent from its IPO.[11]

When a retail channel undergoes such remarkable change, it is extraordinarily difficult for organizations to make informed strategic decisions. Even from a tactical perspective, these rapid changes, which trigger equally dramatic changes in consumer behavior and the sources that influence such behavior, make detailed, research-driven advice and empirically supported theory impractical, if not impossible. Therefore, rather than attempting to address the specifics of electronic and omnichannel retailing – which are likely to be out of date before this book is in print – this chapter provides a general set of guidelines to direct strategic thinking about the role of omnichannel shopping in crafting a retail value proposition.

The Advent of Augmented Reality

As omnichannel shopping continues to develop, the world of retail is going through a revolution on a scale that has not been seen since the telegraph and railroad allowed national brands and multi-store retailers to flourish more than 150 years ago. Yet, as much as things have changed in the last two decades, it is clear that the revolution is in its infancy. Consumers are only on the cusp of mass access to "anytime, anywhere" technologies that facilitate a constant connection to a networked world of information.

A glimpse of the future of retailing can be seen in the business of Webkinz. To a large extent, the impact of this product went unnoticed beyond the market of toys for young children. Stuffed animals are not new, but Webkinz toys are different. Each plush toy comes with a code to key into the Webkinz World website. Once the code is entered, the plush toy appears as an online electronic avatar and a short adoption process begins. When the adoption is finalized, the avatar takes up residence in its one-bedroom virtual home. From there, the children – and in many cases their parents – can begin to accumulate KinzCash, a virtual currency that can be spent at the W Shop. This online store sells a wide variety of virtual items, from furniture to clothing to food, for the Webkinz pet.

With each new Webkinz pet the child acquires and adopts online, another room appears in the virtual home. It is not at all uncommon for children to have dozens of virtual pets living in adjoining rooms within their large virtual house. The pets can play with the children and with each other. Friends in the real world can arrange "play dates" for their pets in the virtual world. The graphics of Webkinz World are not particularly sophisticated and interactions are often slow, but what makes this world special – and especially important for the future of retailing– is that the physical plush toy becomes an interactive pet that is part of a virtual family, shares an online home, and interacts with the virtual avatars of other Webkinz toys from around the world.

Three years after Ganz launched Webkinz in 2005, the line was valued at more than $2 billion.[12] Millions of children belong to the online community. To keep their membership active, they have to buy another Webkinz every twelve months or upgrade their online account to a fee-based deluxe membership. In a relatively short period, Ganz created one of the great modern toy brands and a business model that generates high levels of loyalty and ongoing revenue for years after the initial purchase.

In contrast to other virtual worlds, such as Second Life, World of Warcraft, and Club Penguin, Webkinz is not a toy with a website or a website with a toy, but a product that was developed in both the physical and virtual worlds as an integrated business. This is an important part of the revolution in retailing that Webkinz represents, but it is not the most important part of the story. Webkinz is a turning point in how retailers interact with their customers because Ganz introduces augmented reality to children shortly after they have learned to walk and talk. Toddlers use their own tiny hands, a fraction of the size of their computer mice, to control virtual world avatars and interact with a product in cyberspace. In much the same way that baby boomers grew up with television, today's youngest consumers are growing up in a world that integrates physical and virtual reality. Webkinz is a niche product, and may prove to be a passing fad. Yet, it is a clear illustration of the potential of augmented reality to change the way shoppers interact with the products they purchase.

More generally, the expectations that consumers have for technology as part of the shopping experience are rapidly evolving. Today, we increasingly augment our physical lives with electronic experiences. Examples range from global positioning system (GPS) navigation devices in cars to in-store kiosks for Internet orders to mobile devices that allow consumers to retrieve online product reviews and competitors' prices while shopping in-store. Emerging and early-stage technologies from Google Glass to Apple's iWatch to Occulus Rift promise more immersive, always-on, and wearable devices that connect consumers to apps and the Internet wherever they might be. Augmented reality is no longer science fiction; it is an integrated part of the shopping experience.

An initial effect of consumers' easy access to information and omnichannel shopping is what has come to be known as showrooming – that is, the process of examining products in a retail store but then making the purchase online and having the items shipped directly to the consumer's home. This has been a disruptive practice for several major retailers. It is also the basic business model for companies like Apple and Restoration Hardware. Apple sets up its store to allow shoppers to interact with and experience the different products that it sells. Apple "Geniuses" are happy to provide information and assistance to customers in the store. Yet that investment in real estate, inventory, and employees has not deterred Apple from sending those customers to its website to make the purchase. Not only do they not discourage in-store shoppers from buying through other channels, they actively promote it. Restoration Hardware takes this idea further and considers its physical locations to be "galleries" rather than traditional stores. Guests in the gallery can see and feel the products, but when they want to buy something, store employees help them make the purchase on an iPad, and the product is shipped to the customer's home. Restoration Hardware has intentionally built augmented reality into its purchase process, bridging the real and virtual worlds to improve the brand experience.

Although for most of us this is a novel view of how consumers, product manufacturers, and retailers interact, companies such as Ganz and Restoration Hardware are making these virtual interactions seem completely normal for a new generation of consumers. Those experiences are shaping their expectations for future interactions with retail products.

How Should Retailers Respond?

The good news is that the generation that has grown up with early experiences in augmented reality is still more than a decade away from making the major spending decisions that determine the distribution of retail revenue. Yet the cautionary tales of the print and music industries demonstrate the perils of reacting and reorganizing after consumer behavior has changed. A better approach is that of the grocery and automobile industries, which continue to experiment, plan, and prepare for an evolving customer base. To address this issue, retailers should start by asking, "Will my customers use interactive electronic media more or less over the coming decade?" For most retailers, the answer is clearly more. The next question is, "To what extent will those customers engage as omnichannel shoppers to buy products and services?"

In the long term, it seems likely that every product category will have some portion of sales directly through an electronic channel. There was a time when many experts believed that particular products would always be sold almost exclusively in-store and in person. It was difficult to imagine buying shoes, for example, without ever having touched them or tried them on. Then, in 1999, Zappos began to sell shoes online and grew to over $1 billion in sales within a decade, before Amazon acquired it. Jewelry is another product category that was presumed to require personal sales and visual inspection before a purchase could be made. Yet Walmart, Costco, and Blue Nile have all built strong online businesses selling engagement rings and other jewelry. Consumers report that they appreciate the convenience of buying online and value the easy access to detailed product information, especially product reviews that are generated by their peers. Deeply ingrained shopping routines and consumption patterns do not change overnight, but the trend is clear: consumers want to buy more online and spend less time navigating to stores and negotiating product displays. In the long term, this desire is likely to generalize beyond an online versus physical preference to an expectation of truly ubiquitous shopping and consumption via whatever channel is the most convenient for a particular consumer at a particular place and time.

ESE Omnichannel Retailing

New technologies continue to disrupt the marketplace, making predictions about the future of omnichannel retailing precarious. Nevertheless, the three ESE components of a retail value proposition provide a systematic approach to thinking about the impact of new technology and the nature of the strategies likely to be most effective.

First, how urgent the need for a full-blown interactive electronic sales channel is depends on the *customer segments* the retailer targets. For example, older customer segments are less likely to demand an electronic interface. Yet even among senior citizens, a growing number of customers want to buy online in some product categories. Similarly, retailers that have developed strong personal relationships with their customers and designed a shopping experience around service and an inviting in-store environment are better positioned to defend sales against online competition. In Part 4 of this book, I go into greater detail on the types of measures and metrics that retailers can use to analyze the distribution of satisfaction within their customer base. This can provide a strong signal of the extent to which the retailer's value proposition continues to be relevant and appealing to key consumer segments.

The second question is about *competition*. Are there powerful competitors within the industry that are capable of serving key segments through electronic channels? Take groceries as an example. Many different business models for online grocery stores have been attempted. Some, such as Peapod, Streamline, and Webvan, have failed spectacularly and destroyed billions of dollars in invested capital. Other niche players in categories such as organic food have carved out small businesses that continue to struggle to have a substantial impact on grocery buying. More recently Amazon Fresh has made a major push into online grocery retailing with same-day delivery in some centers. Many pundits are skeptical after the high-profile failures of the past, but outside the United States there have been some major successes.

In the United Kingdom, Tesco has built a thriving online business that now extends to a large number of product categories. Leveraging the strength of the company's traditional bricks-and-mortar grocery business, Tesco was able to offer a profitable Internet shopping experience that captured more than 40 percent of the total market for online grocery shopping in the United Kingdom.[13] In other product categories, retailers are under immediate pressure from competitors that sell primarily through electronic channels. Some companies – such as Nordstrom, Macy's, Walmart, and Target – appear to be making the transition to omnichannel retailing. Others, such as Blockbuster and HMV, have failed to remain relevant to their rapidly evolving customer bases. In deciding to invest in interactive electronic shopping, retailers need to keep a close eye on current and emerging competition within their own industries.

Third, from the perspective of the *environment*, the retailer needs to ask itself whether or not an online presence has the potential to substantially improve the comfort and convenience of the shopping experience. Macy's, a leader in the transition to omnichannel shopping, explains it this way: "Research has shown that about two-thirds of all shopping trips today start online with customers researching the options at their desktops or on smartphones or tablets. Then, the customers often come into the store to touch, feel and try-on the merchandise they saw. Maybe they buy in the store. Or maybe they buy the item later while sitting at home in the evening. We are now operating the company with a single view of our customer, inventory and business – no matter how, when or where the customer is shopping."[14]

Over time this is likely the approach that many retailers will take. As a result, it will become increasingly difficult for a retailer to create a competitive consumption experience without a compelling omnichannel shopping experience.

The fourth question that retailers need to ask themselves is how omnichannel shopping is likely to affect *product selection* in their business. I address product assortments and category management in chapters 6 and 7, but at this stage it is worth noting that adding electronic channels to a traditional store environment can significantly change how a retailer thinks about product selection. As I discussed in chapter 3, a retailer's in-store selection is constrained by the physical space available to display products. This limitation can be alleviated, and possibly even eliminated, when products are sold through an electronic interface. The customer segment targeted by a particular physical store can be more precisely defined without surrendering the ability to serve consumers looking for unique products, unusual sizes, or customized offers. This is the model adopted by companies like Apple and Restoration Hardware. Staff can help shoppers decide what they need and then redirect those looking for customized products, or less common configurations, to an online store to finalize the purchase. Similarly, a modern BMW dealership sells few cars right off the showroom floor. Instead, individual customers tend to use the company's website to build the car they prefer and then work with BMW to acquire or build that particular model. In the world of apparel, retailers struggle to keep the full range of their products stocked in every store at all times yet can offer customers online access to these otherwise unavailable items. As a result, electronic channels can increase sales, profitability, and the number of customers served.

A fifth consideration is whether or not adding electronic channels can substantially improve *customer engagement*. One of the benefits of omnichannel retailing is the ease with which retailers can collect data about customers' attitudes and behaviors. This can happen entirely unobtrusively in electronic channels. For example, a retailer may decide to record how consumers navigate through an electronic store, which products they look at (as well as how often they consider them and for how long), which product reviews they read, and what purchases they make. Even surveys and focus groups seem to appeal more to consumers when conducted through an electronic interface. In fact, many retailers today create panels of their best customers from whom they elicit real-time feedback on everything from logo designs to new product innovations to sales promotions. Companies such as Amazon and Netflix are leaders in using the data they collect about their customers' preferences to make product recommendations. In fact, Netflix has taken the process a step further and begun developing products, such as *House of Cards* and *Orange Is the New Black*, that they know their customers will like.[15] Even retailers who do not see an immediate opportunity for a positive return on investment in electronic commerce must think seriously about how new media can enhance market research and improve customer relationships. I will cover these issues in depth in Part 4 of this book.

Why Retailers Continue to Fear Omnichannel Shopping

Price-Based Competition

One of the lingering fears retailers have about selling in an omnichannel world is the ease with which customers can compare prices and the potential for competition to become entirely price-based. The idea is that because consumers can check competing prices with the click of a mouse, sales dollars migrate to the lowest prices, creating a race toward minimal profit margins.

The problem is that staying offline does not protect you from electronic channel price competition. Amazon's mobile app, for example, has built-in support for scanning bar codes and providing the consumer with both product information and the ability to buy the scanned product from Amazon. This means that if you are looking at a TV in Best Buy you can use your iWatch to scan the bar code or use voice commands to search for the product, and then buy it from your wrist. Omnichannel shoppers are in your stores whether you offer electronic channels or not. The question is: Can they get product information and customer reviews, check prices, and browse alternatives with you or will they be standing in your store shopping with Amazon?

The reality is that the value added by trusted brands, a high level of customer service, efficient delivery, and a familiar shopping environment is even more important in omnichannel shopping. The leading omnichannel retailers, who attract the lion's share of sales and profits, are not competing primarily on price. Even Walmart, the world's most successful low-price retailer, has used its online store to sell higher-priced merchandise. Macy's and Nordstrom's online success is not driven by price. In a virtual world, where shopping is conducted without human-to-human interaction, consumers value retailers they can trust to complete the transaction in a fair and responsible manner. That knowledge derives primarily from the retailer's brand reputation and consumers' prior shopping experiences. As a result, many organizations have found that they have equal, or even greater, pricing power when selling online.

Yet, for those retailers who were counting on consumers' lack of knowledge or high search costs to protect them from competition, omnichannel shopping is a scary thing. Consumers will have more information. They will be able to check prices to ensure that you are not overcharging them relative to the competition. In essence, they will be making buying decisions based on overall value, and retailers will have to be increasingly price competitive in the omnichannel future.

Losing Control of the Conversation

In the era of mass marketing that emerged after the Second World War, retailers became adept at crafting marketing messages. Radio, television, and newspaper advertisements allowed large companies with sufficient resources to broadcast those messages en masse to large segments of the population. Public relations and communications departments worked diligently to ensure that the message was consistent, carefully managed, and integrated with the retailer's strategic position. This approach led to an emphasis on attempting to control – or at least actively manage – the conversation that consumers were having about the company and its brands.

The remnants of this philosophy linger in the boardrooms of retailers that remain hesitant to embrace a strong omnichannel presence because they fear losing control of the conversation. In practice, this is analogous to closing the door after the horse has left the barn. Contemporary customers talk to retailers, product manufacturers, and other consumers on a regular basis. If there was ever a time that a retailer could actively manage consumers' conversations that time has passed. WikiLeaks' and Edward Snowden's release of highly classified government documents from the most powerful nations on earth clearly demonstrated that we live in a world of unprecedented access to information and opinions on even the most tightly controlled conversations.

The good news is that these same technologies have made it easier than ever for consumers to tell their friends about positive experiences, to recommend stores they like, and to rave about products they enjoy. The bad news is that when customers have negative experiences, which can range from poor service and faulty products to inconvenient store hours and long checkout lines, they can also quickly disseminate that information. In Part 4 of this book, I discuss strategies designed to facilitate positive experiences and mitigate the damage of negative interactions. Whether retailers actively engage with customers in an omnichannel environment or not, it is unrealistic to expect to control the conversation. However, companies can actively manage the value they offer and, ultimately, that is what consumers will be talking about.

Losing Focus on the Customers Who Count

Another commonly expressed fear in expanding to retail channels beyond the physical store is that the retailer will lose its focus on its core customers. In fact, study after study has demonstrated that a retailer's most valuable customers are those who actively shop with the retailer through multiple channels.

The shopping environment beyond the physical store has been an important part of the value proposition since Montgomery Ward sent his 1,000-plus-page catalog out to more than 700,000 customers in the late 1800s. It is possible that at some point in the future, electronic shopping channels will account for more business than physical stores. Alternatively, e-commerce may always be a channel that supplements, rather than supplants, bricks and mortar. What is clear is that online, mobile, and other electronic shopping channels are a critical part of the consumption process, and omnichannel retailing is growing at an exceptional rate.

The key to success is experimentation. For some small businesses, online activity may consist of a website promoted through search engine advertising. Others might find more success as active members – or even advertisers – in social networks. The three pillars of environment, selection, and customer engagement are as relevant to an electronic environment as they are to the physical world.

Measuring Success

Similarly, the measures retailers use in online environments are analogous to those they use in physical environments. Revenue, profitability, and return on investment are of critical importance regardless of the sales channel. Traffic and conversion rates remain key metrics for the online retailer. However, in an electronic environment, retailers are often able to get a more fine-grained measure of how many people visit the store, what parts of the store they look at, what products they search for and examine, how long they spend in each area, and how they navigate. Retailers can gather all of these behaviors in an unobtrusive manner, correlate them with conversion rates, and use them to improve the electronic interface – whether that interface is a website, mobile device, smartphone, tablet, or some other virtual connection to the customer. These *behavioral* measures can be used to model the preferences of individual consumers or segments of shoppers.

PART 3

Product Selection

Chapter Six

Buying and Merchandise Management

In the first part of this book, I outlined the importance of the shopping *environment*. The shopping environment is critical and can have a profound influence on the consumption experience. Location, format, and channel decisions go a long way toward defining how comfortable and convenient the shopping experience will be, which in turn can have a direct impact on retailers' revenue and profitability. The environment is the context in which retail happens, but it is not *what* happens.

What happens is the process of consumers choosing products and services from the selection the retailer offers for sale. *Selection* is the second ESE component of the retail value proposition, and the focus of chapters 6 and 7. In the long term, both the shopping *environment* and customer *engagement* are central to the success of a retail enterprise. In the short term, however, the merchant's management of product selection drives performance. For many retailers, making the right product selection decisions is the difference between success and failure. Having the right product at the right time can drive legendary retail performance. Consider, for example, the impact of the e-books for Amazon, espresso for Starbucks, or yoga pants for lululemon. In contrast, selling the wrong products – or the right products at the wrong time – can devastate even the most revered retailers.

The Master Merchandiser

There are few stories that rival Millard (Mickey) Drexler's in North American apparel retailing. In 1983, after Drexler led a successful turnaround at Ann Taylor, he was hired by Gap. At the time, Gap was known as a Levi's retailer that had grown from its entrepreneurial roots in 1969 to become a chain of stores with $480 million in sales.[1]

Drexler is widely credited with completely redesigning the look and feel of Gap stores and rebuilding the product line from scratch to focus on the affordable staple clothing that quickly became the foundation of the North American wardrobe.[2] Drexler also introduced very successful advertising campaigns built on "Individuals of Style" (from Spike Lee to Lorraine Bracco) and "Who Wore Khakis" (with Andy Warhol and Marilyn Monroe). Under his direction, Gap shattered the myth that fashionable, good-quality clothing had to be expensive and built the largest specialty apparel company on the continent.

Realizing that even Gap could not be everything to everyone, Drexler focused the company on the twenty-five- to thirty-five-year-old market and introduced new retail banners to expand into other segments – ranging from children's clothing (GapKids and BabyGap) to lower price points (Old Navy) to higher fashion (Banana Republic).[3] With each move into new markets, Drexler demonstrated an uncanny ability to predict and lead major trends in apparel.

However, after almost two decades of record-setting growth in revenue and profitability, the turn of the millennium was not kind to Drexler or Gap. In response to competition from other specialty retailers (such as Abercrombie & Fitch and American Eagle) and mass merchandisers (including Target and Walmart), Drexler repositioned the product line away from its historical focus on wardrobe basics toward a more aggressive set of styles that included cropped T-shirts, low-rider pants, and bright colors. The company struggled with the new line of clothes, which were not well received by consumers or critics. Those product choices were blamed when Gap lost more than two-thirds of its stock market value.[4] The man who had been widely regarded as the apparel industry's master merchandiser scrambled to recover and was abruptly fired in 2002. The following day, in recognition of Drexler's enormous impact on Gap over the past two decades, investors knocked more than 15 percent off the company's stock price. Under Drexler's leadership, the company had grown from a small apparel chain to over $14 billion dollars in sales across more than 4,200 stores.

Such damage to an iconic company with a long-term record after only a couple of seasons of poor product choices shocked some observers. Yet, that is the reality of selection decisions. Great real estate, a powerful brand, and strong customer relationships are not enough to offset poor product choices. Consistently making the right product decisions is critical to success, and many retailers have built their organizations around a systematic process of buying merchandise.

Retail Buying

It is not uncommon to hear retailers refer to themselves as merchandisers, and many of the country's most successful retailers, from Walmart to Target and from Home Depot to Costco, drive performance through outstanding product management. To be successful, retailers need to develop a system that allows them to make initial strategic decisions, implement those decisions in the details of the buying process, manage the logistics of getting the selected product to stores, and efficiently measure performance in a manner that provides actionable feedback for the next buying cycle.

Figure 6.1 provides a sample organizational structure for a typical retailer. In this style of buying organization, executives at the top of the organizational chart, in consultation with purchasing directors and buyers, make strategic decisions about the portfolio of products the retailer carries. Those decisions tend to fall into three general categories: product assortment, branding, and sourcing.

While consumers think about the selection of products available to purchase, retailers think about the assortment of products they offer for sale. Specifically, product *assortment* refers to the variety, breadth, and depth of the portfolio of products and services the retailer sells.[5] *Variety* refers to how many product categories a retailer uses. For example, a sporting goods company might break its assortment into three general categories: apparel, footwear, and equipment. It could further divide those categories into subcategories – for instance, footwear could become men's, women's, and children's product groupings. If a store sells a large number of different products within each subcategory, it might further classify the products in terms of specific activities – for example, basketball, football, soccer, running, tennis, and so on. How many categories a retailer divides its business into depends on two major factors: the number of products and the target market segments.

In general, when retailers make selection decisions, they group products into categories to help organize the items they want to buy. When the number of products makes detailed buying decisions overly difficult or complex, categorization can help simplify the process. In addition, a retailer may choose to define a specific group of products as a category when those products are particularly important to a key target segment. For example, if a sporting goods store decides to make gender an important criterion in its market segmentation, it is likely to subcategorize footwear by gender even if the number of products in women's

Figure 6.1. Sample Retail Organizational Structure

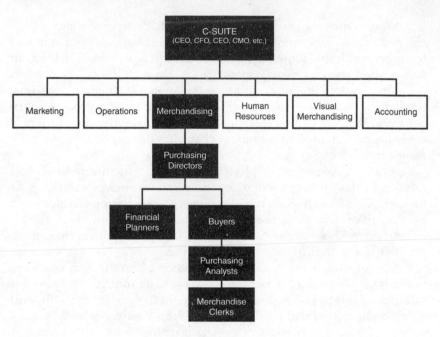

footwear would not, on its own, justify a separate category. As a general rule, large stores operate in many product categories, while small stores operate in only one. Variety describes the number of different product categories that the retailer manages.

The *breadth* of an assortment refers to the number of different products being offered for sale within each category. Some retailers have only a few categories but many different products for sale within those categories. For example, a coffee shop may sell only two categories of products: coffee and related accessories. However, within the coffee category it may offer thousands of different beverages. Starbucks, for example, sells more than 3,500 different coffee drinks in its stores. In contrast, convenience stores tend to have a lot of variety but offer only a few different types of products within each category. For example, a convenience store might sell fresh coffee, but only offer consumers a choice of caffeinated or decaffeinated.

The *depth* of the assortment refers to how many of each individual item the retailer carries. A shallow assortment suggests the retailer has only a few of each stock keeping unit (SKU) it sells, whereas a deep assortment indicates the retailer has a large number of each item in stock. On one hand, deep assortments are expensive, because the retailer must tie up capital in products that sit on the shelf or in the back room. On the other hand, shallow assortments increase the risk of "stock-outs" – that is, running out of a particular item and not being able to offer it for sale until it can be reordered and replenished. In general, retailers want to avoid stock-outs because they can disrupt loyal consumers' shopping patterns by driving them to switch to a substitute product within the same store or (of greater concern) to a competitor's store to purchase the out-of-stock product. Moreover, stock-outs tend to reduce consumers' satisfaction with the retailer, which negatively affects both revenue and profitability in the long term.

It is unrealistic for a retailer to expect to be able to create a perfect or ideal product selection that meets all the needs of all the segments it serves at all times. As part of the strategic planning process, retailers have to decide what risks to take. The company's understanding of the needs of the consumers and its plans to position itself within its target segments should drive the product variety it offers. Beyond variety, managing breadth and depth requires trade-offs. As the retailer expands the breadth of its product selection, the consumer has more choice, but the retailer must manage more individual SKUs and deal with more suppliers. A deep assortment helps avoid the pitfalls associated with stock-outs but can require significant resources and reduce the retailer's ability to invest in other areas, including the shopping environment and customer engagement. Although not an entirely satisfactory solution, electronic retailing has helped to alleviate the problem of stock-outs at the individual store level. The retailer can carry a shallow assortment of products within each store and, if stock-outs occur, refer customers to its e-commerce website to complete the purchase. Apple Stores, for example, have a limited breadth and depth of products onsite, supplemented by a broader, deeper, and customizable product selection available through Apple's website. Restoration Hardware takes an even more extreme "gallery" or "showroom" approach, with few products available for sale directly in the store and almost all ordering done through an electronic interface. Examples of assortment strategies adopted by different retailers are outlined in table 6.1.

Table 6.1 Product Assortment Examples by Variety, Breadth, and Depth

Retail Formats	Variety	Breadth	Depth
Walmart Supercenter	Very High	Wide	Deep
7–11 Convenience Store	High	Narrow	Shallow
Costco	High	Wide	Medium
Starbucks	Low	Very Wide	Very Deep
Apple	Low	Narrow	Shallow
Restoration Hardware	Low	Narrow	Near zero

SKU Level Execution

Variety, breadth, and depth are the parameters of an assortment strategy that define the type of inventory a retailer buys at a general level. However, two stores competing in the same number of categories with the same breadth and depth in their assortment can still occupy very different strategic positions. One approach is through vertical differentiation based on price points; consider, for example, the different positions of men's suits at the following retailers: Tom Ford, Macy's, and Men's Wearhouse. Retailers with similar variety, breadth, and depth in their product assortments may also differentiate themselves horizontally on product attributes such as brand name or style, as is the case between Gap, American Eagle, and Abercrombie & Fitch.

Buyers select the products at the level of individual items or SKUs to deliver on the company's strategic objectives. In organizations that have been selling similar product assortments over many years, the buyer is also able to examine historical sales trends to see what has worked and what has not. Prior years' sales reports can be broken down to classify products as winners or losers, basic items versus specialty items, fads versus staples, and so on. For items that have stable sales trends over time – for example, basic products such as black running shorts in a sporting goods store – the buyer can simply apply a growth rate to the last year's sales to determine how many products to order. If the retailer sold 10,000 black running shorts last year and predicts sales growth of 3 percent – based on prior years' sales, industry trends, economic conditions, and so on – then the buyer will order 10,300 black running shorts for this year.

Sales of other products are not as stable from year to year. For these items, the buyer still considers the available market research, industry data, and economic conditions; however, it is substantially more difficult (if not impossible) to make accurate projections for products that have a lot of variance in year-to-year sales. In such cases, buyers have to rely on their own intuition. Similarly, it is harder to make projections for new products that do not have a track record of sales, as well as products that are significantly affected by rapidly changing fashions and consumer preferences. In addition, the buyer has to consider how the retailer's portfolio of products compares to those of the competition. As a result, even the most sophisticated buying systems often come down to the judgment and intuition of the buyers who select the specific items in the final product assortment. Ordering only skinny ties in a wide-tie year or too much merlot when consumers' tastes turn toward pinot noir can dramatically and adversely affect both revenue and profitability. Moreover, as Mickey Drexler and Gap came to realize, even a decades-long record of making the right assortment decisions within a sophisticated buying organization does not guarantee that the next season will be a success. Merchants are only as good as their last product choices.

Trickle-Down Trend Management

The ability to anticipate major trends in consumer behavior can be extremely valuable to retailers. This is especially true when a retailer is able to predict a change in fashion or identify an emerging trend before the competition does. In general, trends come from one of two directions: they *trickle down* from high-social-status consumers or they *trickle up* from subcultures.

In some cases, trends trickle down from people of high social status in an incidental manner. For example, celebrities often have a substantial impact on consumers' style preferences and popular fashions. The hairstyles of high-profile actors and musicians, for instance, are often quickly adopted within the broader population – from Justin Bieber's "the Bieber," a variant of the Beatles' mop-top, to *Friends* star Jennifer Aniston's "the Rachel" and *Charlie's Angels* star Farrah Fawcett's "the Farrah." Similarly, baby names tend to trickle down from high socio-economic status groups to other parents within the broader population.[6]

Trickle-down trends, however, are not always incidental. Sponsors actively encourage high-profile celebrities to adopt, model, or speak on behalf of products, services, or causes in an effort to intentionally cause a trickle-down effect. Classic examples include Michael Jordan's affiliation with Nike and, in particular, the Air Jordan shoe. More recently, snowboarder Shaun White has been very influential as a spokesperson and celebrity endorser for a variety of products in the youth market.[7] In fact, modern sports marketing is built on a celebrity endorsement model pioneered by Adidas and later perfected by Nike.[8]

Through this type of endorsement, retailers hope to connect their products and services with the positive characteristics of the celebrity. This was a big part of the success of the advertising campaigns that Mickey Drexler introduced at Gap. The company's credibility as a fashion apparel leader intensified through its association with icons ranging from Andy Warhol to Spike Lee to Marilyn Monroe. More recently, the role of spokesperson has been adapted to social media as companies actively recruit – and in some cases generously compensate – high-profile bloggers, Twitter accounts, and Facebook pages to promote products, services, and ideas online.

Although trends that trickle down from high-status groups can have a powerful effect on consumer decisions, such changes in popular styles and fashions are often fickle and short-lived as new celebrities grab the public's attention. In addition, organizations are increasingly concerned about the negative impact that the poor choices and bad behavior of celebrity endorsers can have on the brands they represent. Tiger Woods is probably the best-known example in this regard. Arguably one of the top celebrity endorsers in history, Woods was associated with sponsorships that included not only Nike golf products but also a large variety of commercial interests unrelated to golf – ranging from Accenture Consulting and Buick automobiles to Tag Heuer watches and Gillette shaving products. However, after the high-profile collapse of his marriage as a result of repeated infidelity, many (though not all) of his record-setting sponsorship deals were terminated and marketers everywhere began to rethink the risks of celebrity endorsement. Lance Armstrong suffered a similar fate when, after years of denying doping, he finally admitted that he had cheated to win seven Tour de France titles and lost all credibility as a celebrity endorser.

Rather than try to predict which fashions will trickle down next or attempt to manage trends through celebrity endorsement deals, some retailers adopt a "wait and see, then produce" approach to capitalizing on the trickle-down process. Industria de Diseño Textil of Spain has used this strategy to build the world's largest specialty apparel retailer. More commonly known as Inditex and recognized for Zara, its flagship chain of retail stores, the company is a master of *fast fashion* apparel retailing. Rather than trying to predict trends, fast fashion retailers wait to see what celebrities popularize and which apparel fashions emerge from major industry events, such as fashion weeks held in London, Paris, Milan, and New York. They then rely on a rapid turnaround between identifying the initial design and putting the final product on the shelf to ensure they are early to market with the hottest products. The key to success for fast fashion retailers is maximizing efficiency throughout the supply chain, from product design and manufacturing to shipping and shelf-space management. When effectively executed, fast fashion retailing can take a lot of the risk out of trend management.

Trickle-Up Trend Management

A different approach to trend spotting and trend management is to carefully observe the emergence of trends from niche markets before they *trickle up* to mainstream audiences. Many such trends have affected consumer behavior, from the music industry – including country, punk, and hip hop – to movements grown out of subcultures that range from surfing and yoga to human rights and environmental activism. In general, retailers try to identify these trends and incorporate them into their product selections as they make the leap from niche to mainstream markets.

This is not an easy task, because a retailer has to be able to identify both the trends that will eventually extend into the mass market and the right time to introduce related products. There are many examples of companies that failed as pioneers in markets they entered too early, only to watch similar products later achieve mass appeal and financial success. Examples ranging from tablet PCs before the iPad to espresso coffee houses before Starbucks show that accurately predicting demand for new products from niche markets is a precarious business.

In a historically less common approach, recently retailers have reached out to relevant subcultures to build relationships that benefit both themselves and early adopters in niche markets. An example of this approach is lululemon's work within the yoga community. As a deliberate part of its strategy from day one, lululemon connected with local yoga studios and provided instructors with complimentary clothing. The basic idea is very similar to the approach used by retailers that sponsor celebrity endorsers, whereby the retailer provides the product to the celebrity and hopes it will trickle down and be adopted by mainstream consumers. However, with the subculture community-based approach, the idea is that when more casual yoga practitioners see instructors wearing the clothing, the styles will trickle up to the mass market. Lululemon credits its focus on creating products that appealed to, and were quickly adopted by, leaders in the yoga community as a key factor in its rapid growth.

Other retailers have taken a similar approach to creating communities of consumers built around enthusiasm for particular categories of products and services. For example, Amazon has integrated customer comments and reviews into its shopping experience to encourage people to talk about what they like and do not like in the products it offers for sale. By focusing on "average" people who are not well-known celebrities yet have substantial influence among key segments of the population, retailers are collapsing the distinction between trickle-up and trickle-down trends. Modern marketers are beginning to think in terms of networks of people, some of whom are more influential than others and are therefore worth focusing on. Occasionally, those influential people are celebrities who drive trends down to mainstream audiences; but increasingly they are respected members of local communities capable of sparking fashions that are later adopted by mass consumers.

Finally, it is worth noting that when retailers make product selection decisions, it is often possible to experiment with emerging trends without making a large-scale commitment. For example, as the movement toward better eating and, in particular, organic food has trickled up from foodie subculture and down from celebrity chefs, grocery stores have slowly increased the breadth of their organic offerings. In this way, retailers are able to serve the growing demand for products in an emergent category without dramatically altering their overall assortment strategy. However, the downside of a slow and experimental approach is that it opens the door to new entrants who craft a retail value proposition tailored for a growing market segment. As a result, companies such as Whole Foods are able to disrupt the competitive landscape by focusing on what others believed to be a small niche market.

The ability to identify new trends in consumer demand and deliver products designed to meet those evolving preferences can allow established retailers to break into new markets and new retailers to break into established markets. Missing out on or mis-predicting the emergence of new trends can substantially hurt a retailer on key dimensions, including revenue, profitability, brand equity, and customer loyalty. The constant change in consumers' preferences and the regular introduction of new trends in buying behavior ensure that retailers have to continue to adapt, innovate, and keep an eye open for the trends that will define the next sales season.

The Buying Cycle

To further complicate the buying process, many retailers have buying cycles that require decisions to be made six months or more before the product arrives on the shelf. In some cases reorders are difficult or impossible, as products are manufactured at overseas factories that shift their production to a new set of items. To get a sense of the complexity of the purchasing process, let us consider one buying cycle for a retailer making assortment decisions for the next holiday season (i.e., October to December).

The first stage of the process focuses on planning and usually begins as soon as last season's sales numbers are available. The buyers, working with financial planners – and, in many cases, the executive team – begin by reviewing the performance of product categories, individual items, and brands. At the same time, the executive team formulates the retailer's strategic position for the coming year, which includes articulating the goals for the company and the key metrics that will be used to measure performance. By combining historical information with forward-looking strategies, the retailer is able to generate a *pre-market* outline of the products it plans to purchase. In many cases, this is a general shopping list that sets the budget for spending in different categories but leaves out much of the detail about individual products to allow the buyer to exercise discretion in specific purchases.

After the retailer completes the initial planning and develops a pre-market shopping list, it begins the second stage of the process a few months later in the second quarter of the year. At this point, the buyers begin to make specific decisions, down to the level of individual SKUs, about the products they will purchase. They can do this in two general ways. The first is *market buying*, in which retail buyers decide which of the products sold by wholesalers and manufacturers are the best fit for the pre-market shopping list. This stage often involves travel to trade shows and meetings with representatives from the wholesalers and manufacturers. Larger retailers with substantial buying power tend to get more direct attention from consumer packaged-goods companies and other suppliers, while smaller retailers tend to work with wholesalers or buy through trade shows. Over the past decade, it has become increasingly common for retailers and their suppliers to form ongoing partnerships and alliances to improve the performance of the supply chain and ensure that product assortments are designed to meet the needs of key customer segments.

The other general approach to buying products is known as *specification buying*, which is most common for the purchase of private label products that are exclusive to the retailer and are designed in consultation between the retailer and the manufacturer.

Later in the second quarter, after the retailer has made many of the initial decisions about the specific products that will fulfill the relevant criteria, the pre-market shopping list becomes the *post-market* report. At this stage, the buyer is ready to make recommendations back up the organizational chart, where more senior members of the merchandising team can provide guidance and feedback. In many cases, financial planners are also involved to finalize budget numbers and the allocation of funds in light of feedback from the buyers about what is available in the marketplace. Buyers work with suppliers to get product samples and begin to make decisions with regard to the allocation of products to stores, taking into account available floor and shelf space as well as geographic differences in demand and purchasing patterns. The retailer begins to put together detailed plan-o-grams – that is, illustrations or pictures of how products should be displayed on the store shelf – and other plans for product promotion and in-store advertising. By the end of the second quarter, buyers finalize their orders and begin to work out the logistical details of transporting the products from the suppliers to the retailer.

In the final stage of the process – which begins in late September and early October – the merchandise arrives in stores and warehouses. By now the buying team is in the early stages of the holiday season and can more accurately forecast how its product choices are likely to fare in the market. This is also the time that the team makes any final pricing decisions. In addition, it addresses plans and schedules for end-of-season markdowns, sales, promotions, and final inventory management tactics. As the season progresses, the buying team may also have to deal with inter-store transfers and, when possible, reorders for popular items that sell faster than expected. As the holiday season comes to a close, the retailer analyzes what worked (and what did not) and begins to plan for next year.

This scenario is an example of a typical sales cycle for many retail organizations. Of course, each company has its own systems and

procedures for managing the buying process, and the details vary between different sectors in the retail industry, depending on the number
of sales cycles, the speed at which consumers' preferences change, and
the number of times the company turns over its inventory in a year.
Many retail buyers deal with four or more buying cycles, all at different
stages, at any one time. For example, while they begin to plan for the
next holiday season, buyers may be in the midst of managing inventory
arriving for the winter sales season, ensuring that the products purchased for the spring season are being transported as expected, finalizing the purchases for the summer season, and meeting with suppliers
and manufacturers to see what is available for back-to-school shopping.

The role of the merchandising team, and in particular of the buyers
who make the specific product decisions, is critically important to the
success of a retail organization. As a result, buyers' compensation tends
to be heavily influenced by their performance relative to key metrics
such as overall revenue and profitability, as well as specific measures
related to return on investment and inventory turnover.

Brand Portfolio Management

In addition to managing the variety, breadth, and depth of their product assortment, retailers also make critical decisions about the brands
they will carry and how they will source their products. The allocation
of buying dollars and retail sales space to national brands versus private labels is at the heart of such decisions.

As I discussed in chapter 3, when the telegraph and railroad made
it possible for commercial organizations to coordinate activities over
long distances in North America, national brand names quickly rose
to prominence. Companies such as Procter and Gamble, Heinz, and
the National Biscuit Company took advantage of economies of scale to
minimize costs and build demand among an increasingly affluent consumer base. These *national brands* used the emergence of mass media
– television, radio, newspaper, billboards, and so on – to create brand
names that were widely recognized as signals of high quality at fair
prices. These products also began to signal social status, as an increasingly affluent society consumed national brands as symbols of success.
For most of the twentieth century, sales of national brands grew rapidly, and large manufacturers took a command-and-control approach
to dealing with their much smaller retail counterparts, who distributed
the products to consumers.

However, between the 1960s and the 1980s, a few retailers began to grow beyond their regional borders and accumulate substantial gains in size and market power. In the United States and internationally, Walmart, Carrefour, Tesco, Costco, Home Depot, and others began to demonstrate their power in the supply chain. Today, the world's largest retailers are many times the size of the largest manufacturers. More importantly, retailers have aggressively expanded the market share of their own *private label* products. Retailers can own, develop, and manage private label products, which are sometimes referred to as store brands, own labels, house brands, or dealer brands. Private labels are usually sold exclusively through a retailer's own stores. The sales of private label brands seem to have matured in recent years and are now growing at a little over 1 percent per year.[9] The precise numbers vary by product category, however. In the United States, private labels have just under 18 percent of the market share by dollar value.[10]

The Power of Private Labels

Retailers that have their own brands as part of their product mix have the potential to manage both the brand equity of their stores and the brands they sell within their stores. As a result, private labels provide retailers with greater control over their brand image, customer loyalty, and competitive positioning. In many cases, retailers can exercise much more direct control over pricing and profit margins for private label brands. A retailer can also use store brands to control product supply and increase retailer-specific traffic because its brands are exclusive, whereas national brand promotions apply to many different retailers. On the downside, private labels do not benefit from having the manufacturer pay the bulk of the costs of advertising and other brand-building promotions.

Globally, the penetration rate of private label products averages 16.5 percent, but there is a great deal of variation around this mean. The highest market share exists in Switzerland at 45 percent (with Spain and the United Kingdom close behind at 41 percent), while in Egypt the market share is essentially zero (with China, Thailand, Saudi Arabia, and others at only 1 percent). In the middle of the range are countries like the United States (18%), Canada (18%), Ireland (17%), Italy (17%), Australia (21%), and Norway (21%).[11] Although about half of private label sales are driven by "copycat" brands that offer a product similar to the national brand at a lower price, retailers have begun to use private labels to introduce premium or specialty products.[12]

Over time, private label brands have evolved from low-price, low-quality generic products into a broad range of products that present a competitive alternative to national brands at many different levels of price and quality.[13] As a result, the rise of private labels has contributed to the dramatic shift in power between retailers and manufacturers in two ways. First, as retailers add credible private labels to their product selection, their power in negotiations with manufacturers increases because they have the option to allocate shelf space to the private label at the expense of the national brand. As the private label product's sales increase, retailers benefit from greater experience in product development and, potentially, increased cash flow that can be reinvested back into stores' own brands.

Second, the effect that the rise in private label products has on retailers' power in the supply chain affects changes in consumers' perceptions of product quality. Recall that the ability to use economies of scale both to create better quality products and to communicate more broadly the benefits of those products drove, to a large extent, the rise of national brands. Today, consumers regularly choose between national brands and store brands that are side by side on the same shelf. When the private label product is consistently less expensive than the national brand, consumers become increasingly aware of the trade-off they make by spending more for a higher-quality product. At the same time, as consumers try private label products and are satisfied with the experience, their trust in the quality of store's brand grows. Ultimately, this cycle reduces consumers' willingness to pay the price premium the national brands charge. As a result, manufacturers are under increasing pressure to justify their prices at a time when they are losing sales to private label products, and this in turn is reducing their revenue and their ability to invest in the research and development required to deliver a higher-value product.

Overall, research reveals broad-based consumer acceptance of private label products. For example, a global study of supermarket shoppers conducted by ACNielsen[14] found that among American consumers, 75 percent of respondents agree that private labels are a good alternative to national brands and 74 percent agree that private labels are extremely good value for money. However, national brands maintain their advantage in perceived product quality; only 24 percent of respondents believe that private label brands are suitable products when quality really matters.

Managing Customers, Not Brands

The critical importance of the buying process to retail success has led many executives to become obsessed with product and brand management decisions. As the Mickey Drexler story illustrates, making the wrong choices can have severe consequences, and even the strongest retail brands are vulnerable when they lose touch with their customers. Ultimately, retailers should ensure that they have the right products for the customers they aim to serve, rather than try to sell the products they have to whoever walks in the door. This might sound like a subtle distinction, but it is an important one. Too many retail organizations are built around products and brands rather than customers – a strategy that inhibits growth and jeopardizes profits.

To illustrate this point, consider General Motors' management of the Oldsmobile brand. Oldsmobile was a revered automobile brand with a long history in North America. Yet in the last decades of the twentieth century, increased competition and changing consumer tastes resulted in a dramatic decline in sales and profitability. In response, GM decided to try to appeal to younger consumers through a series of advertising campaigns that aimed to associate Oldsmobile with tag lines such as "this is not your father's Oldsmobile" and "a new generation of Olds." That approach failed to turn the tide as the brand declined from 6.9 percent market share to 1.6 percent by the turn of the century and, in December 2000, General Motors announced it would phase the brand out of production.[15]

A large part of the problem was that the company focused on the Oldsmobile brand and its product line rather than on car-buying consumers. The management team asked, "What customers should we sell our products to?" They came up with a very logical and intelligent answer: the younger generation of up-and-coming consumers who are and will continue to be high-value customers. As a result, GM adopted a strategic focus that led to a major commitment to persuading those customers to buy an Oldsmobile. The company could have saved itself a lot of time and money – and pursued other opportunities with the potential for a positive return on investment – if it had asked, "What products do customers want to buy?" The answer would have been: not an Oldsmobile.

Department stores such as JCPenney and Sears have struggled with a similar problem. These retail brands are much stronger than the companies' current customer relationships. JCPenney made a major shift in its product selection under Ron Johnson and has since drifted back to a more traditional assortment. Sears continues to struggle to find a solid position in a market dominated by Target and Walmart. Globally, Target and Walmart, along with other great retail brands like Gap and Starbucks, have seen their fortunes rise and fall as they have been more or less in touch with what their local customers want.

The lesson to be learned from these and many other examples is that rather than building customer segments around brands, brands should be built around profitable customer segments. Put another way, retailers have realized that great customer relationships result in unusual profitability and powerful brands, but powerful brands alone do not create customer relationships capable of driving profitable performance.

The Consumer-Centric Shift toward Cooperation and Collaboration in the Supply Chain

Improved customer-centricity is my focus in the remaining chapters in this book, but it is worth noting here that a first step toward stronger customer relationships and more profitable product assortment decisions is improved cooperation and collaboration between retailers and manufacturers within the supply chain. The reality is that retailers are likely to continue to increase the number of private labels in their product assortments; however, the majority will also continue to carry a broad assortment of national brands. By using a mix of store and national brands, retailers can differentiate their product selection both horizontally and vertically, which allows them to appeal to multiple consumer segments simultaneously.

In fact, research and anecdotal evidence indicate that there can be a substantial negative impact on revenue, profitability, customer loyalty, and bargaining power within the supply chain when a retailer minimizes or entirely removes national brands from its product assortments. In a high-profile example, Walmart was forced to backtrack on a plan to reduce the breadth of its product assortment in several categories. The company believed it could reduce inventory and improve margins by carrying an increasingly narrow selection of national brands and simultaneously expanding Walmart's "Great Value" private label. However, it found that customers were unhappy when it eliminated national brands, even when those particular brands did not sell especially well. Walmart quickly reversed course and reintroduced the national brands after the fourth quarter of 2009, when its revenue declined and market share shrank for the first time in its history.[16]

The mix between private labels and national brands can have a direct impact on a retailer's ability to negotiate with suppliers and manufacturers. In the 2007 book *Private Label Strategy*, authors Nirmalya Kumar and Jan-Benedict Steenkamp argue that although the introduction of store brands initially increases a retailer's power within the supply chain, too many private labels have the opposite effect. Specifically, the authors contend that when a retailer includes well-designed private label products as a part of its assortment, it represents a credible threat to national brands sold in the same category. As a result, the retailer increases its strength in the bargaining process. As additional private labels enter into the mix, the retailer's power continues to rise, but only up to a point. When private label products dominate the assortment, that power diminishes as national brands are forced to look for other means of distribution.

In addition, as the Walmart example illustrates, at some point consumers begin to resent the lack of breadth and become increasingly likely to shop at another store that offers a selection with more choice. Ultimately, the real power belongs to consumers. It is the value of the offering from the perspective of the customer that determines what will sell and what will not. As a result, retailers and manufacturers are becoming less competitive with each other and increasingly collaborative in their efforts to meet the needs and desires of the customers they serve. In chapter 7, I take a closer look at how retailers can work with manufacturers to improve the overall fit between their strategic position and their product selection. Rather than focusing on putting products on the shelf, this approach emphasizes overall *category management* to meet the goals of the retailer by serving the needs and desires of key customer segments.

Measuring Success

The number and type of measures that retailers use to assess the company's buying process, individual buyers, and overall merchandising success are as different as the retailers themselves. As discussed throughout the book, revenue, profit, return on investment, and other high-level information on financial performance should be at the forefront of a retail organization's strategic planning. However, these measures are often too general to evaluate the buying process and are affected by many factors beyond the control of buyers.

To more directly assess the success of the buying and merchandising team, retailers tend to look at results in terms of gross margin, which buyers directly influence through the cost of the products they purchase and the prices at which they sell the products. More specifically, retailers are interested in the gross margin return on inventory (GMROI), which is calculated by dividing the gross margin by the average inventory cost. The gross margin captures both the wholesale price that the buying team negotiates and the retail price at which the products are sold. The average inventory cost is the money the retailer has tied up in the products that are sitting on store and warehouse shelves, averaged over a specific period. How quickly products sell and how efficiently products are delivered from suppliers directly affect that number. GMROI provides a snapshot overview of the entire buying process in a single metric, and so it has become a popular measure of merchandising success.

In addition to GMROI, many retailers look specifically at inventory turns, sell-through, and stock-outs. *Inventory turns* refers to the number of times that the inventory is sold per period (e.g., number of times the store's inventory is turned over per year). *Sell-through* looks at how quickly merchandise sells in comparison to what the buying team expected. It is calculated as follows:

Sell-through = (sales – inventory purchased) / inventory purchased

or

Sell-through = (actual sales – planned sales) / planned sales

When sell-through is a negative number, the merchandise is not selling as quickly as expected and price discounts may be required. When sell-through is a positive number, the merchandise is selling faster than expected and the retailer is at risk of a *stock-out*. A stock-out occurs when a store sells its entire inventory of a particular product and consumers who want to buy the product are unable to do so – that is, the product is out of stock. Stock-outs are important to monitor because they represent a lost sales opportunity and disappoint and dissatisfy customers.

Finally, many retailers want their merchandising teams to consider how buying decisions affect the retailer's return on investment in real estate. Gross margin return on space (GMROS), which is calculated by dividing the gross margin by the cost of the space (square footage) used to sell the relevant products, can be helpful in this regard.

Integrating Metrics into Management

In the first half of this book, I focused on the environment and selection components of the retail value proposition. Each of the initial six chapters concludes with a section on measuring success, which outlines a set of common metrics that have been used to assess retail performance. These metrics have served retailers well during the past several decades as American stores have dramatically expanded in size and complexity to accommodate the proliferation of globally sourced products demanded by consumers. Merchandising and the management of real estate have defined competition during this period.

In the second half of the book, my focus is on the component of the retail value proposition that will define the next era of competition: customer engagement. Beginning with chapter 7, the environment and selection components become increasingly integrated with customer engagement. In the following chapters, I apply the concepts discussed so far to progressively more fine-grained approaches to segmentation that push retailers to think in terms of individual consumers. As a consequence, the important metrics evolve beyond simply evaluating past performance and begin to inform the practices of forward-looking retailers – that is, key metrics become an integral part of strategic retail management. Therefore, rather than concluding each chapter with a summary of important measures, the second half of the book incorporates consumer analytics into the design of the retail value proposition.

Chapter Seven

Category Management

American retailers are in the fortunate position of being able to buy products from a large number of manufacturers in many categories. If none of those products is exactly what they want, retailers can design their own private label store brands. However, this wealth of choice means that retailers have some tough decisions to make, including:

- Which products and brands should be carried within the category?
- How much floor space should be given to the overall category?
- How much space should be allocated to the different products/ brands within the category?
- Which products/brands should get the premium display space?
- How should the products be organized within the category (type, brand, segment)?
- How much of the advertising budget should be allocated to each category and to the individual brands within each category?

In addition, for every category the retailer decides to compete in, it will have to manage relationships with suppliers and manufacturers and ensure that the products it offers for sale meet consumers' demands. These decisions are dynamic and time sensitive – the retailer has to get the timing right on trends that emerge, expand, and fade with little notice. This process can be overwhelming, especially for retailers that manage many large-format stores that carry tens of thousands of individual products in a large variety of categories.

Consider, for example, the relatively straightforward category of bicycles. Before the spring arrives, companies such as Walmart, Dick's Sporting Goods, Costco, Target, Sears, and many others commit substantial floor space to the bicycles they hope to sell in the spring season. As I discussed in chapter 6, they have made decisions about the breadth and depth of their assortments many months earlier, and the products they have chosen to offer for sale go a long way toward defining their market positions. Walmart, for example, tends to vertically differentiate its bicycles by offering entry-level products at low prices. Dick's Sporting Goods is vertically differentiated from Walmart by offering higher quality products at a higher price. Although there is some additional subtle price-based differentiation between Walmart, Target, and Sears, they tend to compete primarily through horizontal differentiation – that is, offering a series of different brands within a similar range of prices. Local specialty shops tend to vertically differentiate the market further by selling more expensive bike brands and occupying a higher price-quality market position.

Each of these bike retailers can arrange products in a large variety of ways. Products can be grouped by type (e.g., road versus mountain versus hybrid bikes), by brand, or by target segment (e.g., children's, men's, women's, etc.). The retailer has to decide which bikes get the premium floor space, with more traffic and easier consumer access, and which are farther back in the store, hung from the ceiling, or stored in a back room or warehouse. It also has to allocate advertising dollars toward certain products, brands, or segments, as it grapples with limited budgets and consumers who are bombarded with advertised offers from many different sources.

The complexity of the buying process, ever-evolving consumer preferences, and intense competition make these decisions extremely difficult for the retailer who approaches product management in an ad hoc fashion. To effectively manage a modern retail enterprise, merchants need to have a strong consumer-centric strategy for the company, the store, the categories within each store, and the individual products within each category. This approach to merchandising is known as *category management*, and it has become the process that underlies product decisions for the world's leading retailers.

The Process of Category Management

Building on marketing basics, category management treats each product category as an individual business unit that can be customized at the store level to satisfy consumers' needs while simultaneously achieving the retailer's overall strategic objectives. Early in the 1990s, category management emerged as a process designed to minimize the risks inherent in traditional buying systems, which relied too heavily on the merchant's experience and intuition. With the increasing use of category management, the organizational structure evolved to ensure that marketing, merchandising, visual merchandising, and buying worked together as part of a single team to craft, manage, and implement the retailer's assortment strategy on a category-by-category basis (see, for example, figure 7.1).

Companies such as Safeway and Kroger pioneered the process to address the challenges of a grocery industry defined by low margins, intense competition, product proliferation, and demanding consumers. Other types of retailers soon began to adopt similar processes after the grocers demonstrated that by practicing category management they were able to reduce their inventories, increase sales, and build loyalty. Over time, individual retailers have evolved the basics of the category management process to meet their own specific needs, objectives, and organizational structures. Nevertheless, most category management systems are derived from the eight-step process developed by The Partnering Group (TPG)[1] and outlined in figure 7.2.

Category Definition

One of the most important insights of category management is that product categories should be defined by the needs of consumers rather than by the items the store sells. As a simple example, consider a consumer picking up nacho chips to eat with friends while watching a hockey game. A grocery store that builds categories based on product similarity would tend to put the nachos with other salty snacks such as potato chips and pretzels, while grouping complementary items such as salsa and guacamole in a different aisle with other condiments. A hockey-watching consumer, however, would be much better served by a store that placed salsa and guacamole on the shelf beside the nachos. To go even further, the grocery store might include a cooler nearby with a selection of shredded cheeses, sour cream, and ground beef. But what happens to the consumer who wants to buy the same shredded cheese as a pizza or salad topping? Does the retailer have multiple cheese displays throughout the store wherever a consumer might consider it a complementary item?

The key to defining a category is the retailer's segmentation scheme. A local convenience store might very well have a "nachos" category

Figure 7.1. Sample Organizational Structure for a Retailer Using Category Management

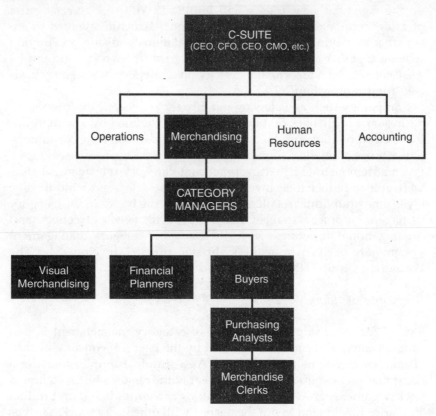

because it aims to serve customers who want a quick and easy way to get snacks for tonight's game. For most grocery stores, it makes more sense to have categories defined as condiments, dairy, and snacks, because consumers' shopping lists are organized to make use of products in each of those categories in multiple ways (e.g., they purchase shredded cheese for pizzas, salads, and nachos).

A critical element of the category management process is to base such decisions on store-level customer data. For example, Kroger might find that, at one of its more urban locations, customers purchase shredded cheese almost exclusively with nachos, salsa, and guacamole. In the same city, Kroger might have other stores where customers purchase

Figure 7.2. The Eight-Step Category Management Process

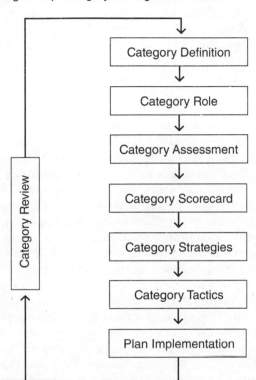

shredded cheese and nachos together only occasionally. It makes sense to create a "nachos" section in the one downtown location but not in the other stores.

Similarly, Walmart's data might reveal that its most loyal and profitable bicycle customers make their first purchase in the category when they buy an entry-level bike with training wheels. This would lead Walmart to give the premium floor and display space to those entry-level products. It might also lead to the most aggressive pricing for those bikes and an advertising campaign concentrated on those entry-level products. In contrast, imagine a different scenario wherein the company's data indicate it tends to primarily sell low-margin bikes to price-sensitive consumers; however, each bike sale comes with several high margin accessory purchases. In this scenario, the category would be organized to feature the most competitively priced bikes while prominently displaying a large selection of accessories. The point is that products alone should not define a category; the needs and preferences of the specific consumers who buy and use those products should define it.

The Category Role

The second step in the category management process is to ensure that each category has a clearly defined role that contributes to the retailer's overall strategic plan. This means that there are as many different category roles as there are corporate objectives. Categories can define the retailer and make it a *destination* store for consumers looking for particular products. For example, a given consumer might think of Sears as a destination for tools and appliances, while considering Target for apparel and Costco for consumer electronics. Although all three retailers compete across many different areas, they can differentiate themselves within specific segments based on the investment in and emphasis on each of those product categories.

Most consumers are reluctant to think about any one retailer as the go-to place for all of their purchases across multiple product categories. In other words, not every category in the store can be the star of the show. Individual retailers choose a specific category – or small set of categories – that defines who they are and then develop other categories with complementary roles. For example, while the electronics destination category might bring consumers into a Costco, they might also sample and purchase a new frozen pizza. The retailer might define frozen food as a *convenience* category, because when people are already in the store for the latest DVD release, it is convenient for them to pick up a pizza at the same time. Similarly, Target might draw in a shopper who wants to buy a Mossimo summer dress and at the same time grab that latest DVD. Such categories are often described as convenience categories – they do not define the retailer, but they do add value to targeted customer segments and improve the overall shopping experience.

Another general role for a product category is to service *routine* or habitual purchases. In some grocery stores, the produce section might fulfill this role. Consumers purchase fruits and vegetables as a routine part of a grocery shopping trip. It is important for the store to offer this product category, because it is an important part of the basket of goods the grocery shopper buys on a regular basis. The grocery store might focus on offering consistent good-quality produce, but in this example that would not be the reason why consumers choose this store over others. A different grocery store could use produce as a destination category. It is not the products sold that determine the category's role; instead, it is the retailer's overall strategy that determines how the products in the category are positioned in the minds of the customers relative to what the competition offers.

Even though routine categories do not define the retailer, they can play an important role in attracting customers to the store and increasing visit frequency within key segments. Walmart, for example, uses its grocery business primarily as a means to draw in more customers more often. Similarly, *seasonal* categories can play an important role in attracting customers to the store at specific times of the year. A bicycle category can generate traffic in the spring and give customers a reason to visit the store as spring and summer products replace winter merchandise. In apparel and other fashion-driven businesses, the arrival of a seasonal category can create excitement and draw consumers back to the retailer.

Category Assessment

An ongoing process of feedback, analysis, and assessment of the categories the retailer has defined is at the heart of category management. Assessment can happen in a variety of ways. It can be based on market-level feedback, such as how the retailer performs – in terms of metrics like sales and profit – in the category relative to the competition. Category assessment could also include an analysis of the relationships within the supply chain. For example, does the category generate enough sales to make it worthwhile for manufacturers to invest in co-operative advertising or to provide the retailer with in-store displays or product demonstrations? Along the same lines, a retailer might assess the balance between private label and national brands offered for sale in the category. Do the returns of the different brands in the portfolio justify their floor space and display prominence?

However, for the consumer-centric retailer, category assessment tends to focus on how effectively that group of products meets the needs of the targeted segments. For example:

- Do the destination categories attract and retain the right customers?
- Which products within the category sell well and which products lag expectations?

- To what extent is the category part of a planned shopping trip versus an impulse buy?
- What is the average amount spent per customer in each category in each of the key segments?
- How quickly is the category growing relative to the overall market and other categories in the store?

These assessments should be conducted within the context of the retailer's overall goals and objectives for the store and the company, and require a combination of empirical data and managerial judgment. The specific data analyses a retailer conducts depend on the strategic position the company has set for itself. However, many retailers practicing category management use a category scorecard to help focus their judgments on a few critical measures.

Category Scorecard

The category scorecard is the set of measures the retailer has identified as being especially important to its business. Some retailers update and review these metrics on a day-to-day basis and compare them to expectations based on the same category's performance in similar stores or year-over-year sales trends in the same store. Other retailers only review the scorecard on a weekly or monthly basis. The depth and detail of the scorecard depend on the sophistication of the retailer's information technology and data management capabilities. More advanced systems may be able to break down the data by segment, including separate reports for customers with the highest predicted value (as discussed in chapter 9). Simpler systems might provide a snapshot based on the company's income statement or balance sheet broken down and reported at the level of individual product categories. The numbers the retailer focuses on should reflect its goals, and can be as simple as category-specific satisfaction surveys or revenue or as complex as the cross-category basket composition by shopping trip within target segments. It is worth noting that a system's sophistication is not a measure of the value of a category scorecard. The critical function of this data collection and analysis is to provide the retailer with accurate and reliable feedback on the performance of the category.

A category scorecard is likely to include many of the basic buying metrics introduced in chapter 5, including GMROI, GMROS, inventory turns, sell-through, and stock-outs – measures that provide insight into how well the category is performing with regard to the retailer's investment in inventory. Similarly, a retailer might want to look at how the category is faring in relation to its other big investments in real estate and employees. In terms of real estate, merchants commonly look at GMROS, revenue per square foot, and (gross and net) profit per square foot. With regard to employees, retailers often consider revenue per employee, profit (gross and net) per employee, and shrinkage (or theft) per employee. Some retailers examine these metrics for each staff member – and even account for external factors such as seasonality, time of day, day of week, relevant promotions, and so on – while others consider only aggregated data. Looking at category performance relative to the major investments the retailer has made in inventory, real estate, and employees can provide some insight into the return it is receiving for those investments. When compared to other categories, similar stores in other locations, competitors, and general industry trends, this information can help the retailer assess the effectiveness of those investments.

The retailer can also use a scorecard to track trends over time in how key customer segments perceive its performance within specific product categories. Relevant measures in this regard can include customer satisfaction, brand equity, the likelihood that the customer will recommend the retailer to others, and the value of specific customer segments. A sophisticated scorecard could allow the retailer to dig deeper into small segments or even individual customers to examine how recently they have made purchases (and how soon the next purchase can be expected), how frequently they visit the store, and how much they spend. Loyalty card data, which I examine in detail in chapter 10, can be especially informative in this regard.

In addition, a retailer might want to look at the revenue, profit, and sales volumes generated by individual products within the category. In many cases, companies find that category sales follow some variant of Pareto's principle – that is, 20 percent of the products within a category account for 80 percent of the sales. This type of analysis can provide the retailer with insight into the value of individual products within the assortment and can inform the placement of products within the store and on the shelves. For example, if Sears finds its Craftsman private label tools account for the majority of sales in its hardware category, it may want to give those products the most prominent displays and feature them in advertising and promotions. Alternatively, Sears may decide it would like to further encourage the purchase of other brands within its assortment to ensure that consumers perceive its assortment breadth to be comparable to what competing retailers are able to offer. Although the retailer's overall strategy should drive the ultimate category management decisions, a well-designed category scorecard can provide critical quantitative input into that decision process.

Category Strategies

A retailer can assign each category a specific marketing strategy or set of strategies in addition to its general role. As with the category role, the retailer's goals and objectives for the store and the entire organization should drive these strategies. Examples of basic category strategies include plans to achieve the organization's goals with respect to generating traffic, improving profit margins, building brands, attracting specific consumer segments, increasing the size of the average sale, servicing routine or convenience purchases, or creating customer loyalty.

To continue with an earlier example, Walmart could use its bicycle category in several different ways. The strategy for the category could be to generate store traffic during the spring and summer seasons. The company could go even farther in that direction with a strategy that aimed to increase traffic among a particular market segment – for example, families with young children. Alternatively, the company could decide that the strategy for the bikes category is to contribute to the store's average profit, which would imply an assortment of higher margin products and less inventory depth. It could also define the category's role as brand building and offer a selection of products with well-known brand names that expand Walmart's appeal. In addition, the company could have subcategory strategies within the overall bicycle category. For example, while the strategy for bikes could be to build traffic, bicycle accessories could be used to increase margins.

Clearly, it is important for the retailer to adopt a strategy for a category that is consistent with the role it has assigned to that category. If Walmart wants to use its selection of bikes as a destination category, its strategy for its bicycle offering should be consistent with its goal of drawing consumers to its stores. The focus should be on building traffic within particular segments and choosing products that differentiate Walmart from its competition – that is, the strategy should be one that attracts the desired customers to the store. If Walmart decides that although the bikes category is important, it is not one of the company's primary points of competitive differentiation, it might assign bikes to a seasonal role. That approach would suggest a focus on selling to customers who are already shopping at the store, rather than using bicycles to entice customers to the store. As a result, the company is more likely to adopt a strategy that aims to accomplish a different set of goals, such as increasing the average amount spent by customers in the store, enhancing customer loyalty, or improving margins. In making decisions about the category's role and the strategy to fulfill that role, the retailer maps out its competitive position within that product market. That is, it decides where and how it competes. Exactly what the retailer does depends on the *tactics* it employs and the effectiveness with which it can implement the complete plan.

Category Tactics

Category tactics are about what the retailer does to ensure that the category is able to fulfill its designated role and meet its strategic goals. At a general level, these tactics touch on each of the ESE components of the retail value proposition – the design of the store environment, selection decisions, and customer engagement – that I address in detail throughout this book. In addition, pricing can be a particularly powerful tactic that retailers can use in support of category-specific strategies that range from generating traffic – through everyday low prices or sales promotions – to improving profit margins.

The important point is that once the retailer determines the category's role and strategic focus, the next step is to choose the specific tactics it will implement in support of those higher-level objectives. To continue with the bikes example, if Walmart decides to use bicycles as a destination category to increase store traffic, that suggests tactics focused on advertising, price promotions, and a product assortment capable of generating inventory turns. If the retailer decides it is a seasonal category that aims to increase the share-of-wallet Walmart earns from its loyal customers, then the category tactics are more likely to focus on in-store promotions and a product assortment tailored to the preferences of key consumer segments. Ultimately, marketing tactics should flow directly from the role and strategy assigned to the category.

Plan Implementation

Up to this point in the process, category management has been strategic planning that treats groups of products as individual business units. The next step is plan implementation. A category management plan builds on the organization's buying process (as described in chapter 6) with an even more detailed schedule of activities and assignment of responsibilities. In particular, unlike the traditional buying processes, category management demands a more collaborative approach to implementation that assigns distinct responsibilities to the retailer's employees as well as to employees who work for partner organizations throughout the supply chain.

The retailer should take the lead in assigning roles and strategies to each of the categories it defines. It should also take responsibility for designing the scorecard and directing the assessment process, including gathering the relevant data and choosing the employee who will ultimately be accountable for decisions made within each category.

However, the process of category management requires information and expertise that most retailers cannot access easily or cost-effectively. National brand manufacturers can play an important role here, as they have a bird's-eye view of trends in consumer product preferences and buying habits across the entire market. Those aggregate level data are an important benchmark against which a retailer can compare its own category performance. In addition, many manufacturers have developed deep expertise in category management that they are willing to share with retailers. The extent to which a retailer can benefit from this expertise varies with the breadth and depth of its internal capabilities. While some retailers need the manufacturer to play only a supporting role, others can benefit from a very close collaboration with their suppliers and even outsource critical roles.

A common example of such collaboration is when the retailer assigns one manufacturer to play the role of *category captain*. When category management was first introduced, manufacturers were quick to offer their assistance to the retailers they supplied (or wanted to supply) with product. As a result, retailers faced several different and conflicting proposals for their categories. To simplify the process, retailers began to appoint one manufacturer to be the category captain – that is, the chief adviser to that specific product category. The other suppliers are still included in the process, but they tend to take on a subordinate role of checking and validating the recommendations of the category captain. The depth of collaboration varies across retailers and manufacturers, from general advice on category trends to detailed plans for product placement on the shelf and promotion within the store. In fact, it is not uncommon for a manufacturer in the role of category captain to assign a team of employees to work with an individual retailer. In some cases, those teams are integrated into the retailer's product management group and work out of the retailer's offices, yet are paid by the manufacturer.

From the retailer's perspective, the category captain must be able and willing to collaborate in a manner that supports the retailer's strategy for both the specific category and its business overall. In addition, a category captain is of little value if his or her advice is biased or ill informed. This can be challenging, as the captain works for the manufacturer but makes recommendations that could give an advantage to that manufacturer's competitors. In addition, the retailer relies on the captain for unique, data-driven insights that give it a competitive advantage. Of course, in many cases, the manufacturer also supplies products to the retailer's competitors and must be careful in how it manages proprietary or confidential information. At the end of the day, the process of category management is an important step toward a more collaborative and less competitive retail supply chain. Nevertheless, there continue to be significant challenges in the tactical execution of well-intentioned strategic plans. Ultimately, category management is an ever-evolving process that works best when it is collaborative and consumer-centric.

Category Review

Much like the buying process, category management requires constant vigilance. On a regularly scheduled basis, the retailer and its key suppliers need to conduct a "SWOT"-style analysis, which looks at the strengths, weaknesses, opportunities, and threats for each category within the store. The retailer's category scorecard is central to the review process. In particular, the retailer needs to ask the following questions:

- How has the category performed on the key metrics the retailer has identified as critical to its success?
- Are those still the right metrics?
- How have different categories within the same store performed relative to one another, and how have the same categories performed across different store locations?

The retailer also looks at how those same metrics stack up relative to the performance of its competitors. In collaboration with suppliers, the retailer asks:

- How has the category performed relative to the competition in terms of key metrics?
- Does the assortment of products reflect the preferences of target segments?

- Do specific tactics – such as pricing, promotion, in-store displays, and so on – need to be revised?

In addition, the retailer reviews previous strategic decisions in light of the new data, including answering questions such as:

- Should the role, strategy, or tactics for the category be revised?
- Is the implementation proceeding as planned?

The results of the category review are then fed back into the first step of the process.

The eight-step process provides a template for category management that individual retailers can tailor to their specific needs. However, in addition to managing product categories, retailers must decide which categories to carry in which stores. In the competitive world of retail, this decision is not always as straightforward as it might seem. Retailers that historically focused primarily on grocery products, for example, have moved aggressively into other product categories such as pharmacy, alcohol, gasoline, apparel, and electronics. Drugstore chains have increased their market share in cosmetics and convenience foods. Hardware stores have moved into home furnishing and appliances.

Ultimately, the focus on the consumer – and in particular, on the key target segments the retailer aims to serve – is the driving force behind product and category management decisions. The categories a retailer chooses to carry in a store, and the products that store offers for sale within those categories, should be determined by who shops there and whom the company would like to have shop there. As retailers began to focus more intensely on creating a consumer-centric and systematic process built on marketing fundamentals, they realized that historical approaches to buying were no longer adequate. For many retailers, this led to a new level of cooperation and collaboration with their suppliers and the management of product categories as individual business units. This approach to assortment decisions pushed retailers to a new level of quantitative analysis and data-driven management. Over time, this evolution has led retailers away from product merchandising and toward an intense focus on small segments of shoppers to gain a competitive advantage. Building on their expertise in designing compelling retail environments and crafting appealing product selections, modern retailers invest heavily in the aspects of their retail value propositions that engage the right customers.

PART 4

Customer Engagement

Chapter Eight

Managing Customer Relationships

As a general rule, retailers are customer focused. As I have discussed throughout this book, good retailers think about the customer segments they serve when they craft a retail value proposition – including the individual decisions around choosing store locations, designing store interiors, developing retail channels, and managing product categories. Yet, most retailers remain merchants at heart – they focus on selling merchandise, rather than managing customers. This is the story of many of the world's most successful and admired companies, from Costco and Home Depot to Starbucks and Apple. Outstanding merchandise management has been a great model for building a retail company, but it is becoming increasingly difficult to drive sustainable growth exclusively through the shopping environment and product selection components of the retail value proposition.

Ultimately, continuing to focus on the shopping environment and product selection alone pushes retailers to deliver ever-improving consumption experiences at lower and lower prices. It is an arms race under the banner of "build it and they will come." Retailers take similar approaches to investing in environments and product selections in the hope that their offering is better than that of the competition. To some extent, this is the nature of capitalism. Strong and increasing competitive pressures drive innovation and provide consumers with more for less. But from the retailer's perspective, such competition is a losing game if the customer is not at the center of the strategy.

Rethinking Retailing

Shopping environments and product selections exist to serve customers. Yet, most retail organizations are structured to manage products. The movement to category management is one example. At the heart of this approach to merchandising is a deep understanding of the customer, but the focus is still on the products. Category managers tend to think about building product selections based on what they know about their customers. They tend not to be customer managers who think about building their clientele based on what they know about their products.

To understand the distinction, it is helpful to think in terms of a single customer – I will call him Bob. When it was time to get his first bike, Bob's parents took him to Walmart. The category manager focused on providing a great selection of bikes to young families like Bob's, and knew a great deal about the families who lived in the store's trading area, including where they liked to ride, what style of bike they preferred, and how much they were willing to spend on an entry-level bike. With this knowledge, the category manager met with several manufacturers and suppliers and even helped develop Walmart's own private label bicycles, designed to appeal to target customers like Bob. Not surprisingly, when Bob's family arrived in the bicycle section they were very satisfied with the selection of products. They easily found a bike Bob liked at a price they were happy to pay. In fact, the experience was so positive that when Bob outgrew his first bike, he insisted they go back to Walmart to buy his next one, and his parents happily complied.

By that time, there was a new category manager responsible for bicycles who had also invested heavily in getting to know the potential customers who lived around the store. He realized that the families in the area were getting older and their bike preferences had changed. Using this information, he worked hard to evolve the product selection, and once again Bob found the perfect bike. A few years later, Bob was a hardcore bicycle enthusiast. Walmart that realized some of the young families it had served in the past five to ten years had children who had grown up to be bike enthusiasts. At the same time, it knew that the enthusiast segment was relatively small and that specialized bicycle retailers were better positioned to serve customers like Bob. Similarly, Bob knew Walmart did not carry the type of bikes he was looking for. Bob still felt very fond of Walmart and recommended the store to friends who were not bike enthusiasts, but he no longer shopped there for a bike himself. From the category manager's perspective, this type of customer evolution was inevitable and simply meant that over the years the store would lose some customers.

By many standards, Walmart and the category manager were extremely customer-centric in the development of the bicycle category.

Nevertheless, their primary focus was on finding customers for the products they sold, rather than finding products for the customers they served. If a customer manager – rather than a category manager – had served Bob and his family, Walmart would have taken the same approach to the bicycle category, but would also have understood that Bob's family's value went far beyond buying bikes. Bob's mother liked to garden; his father liked to spend a lot of time and money working on his 1974 Ford Mustang. Bob spent a lot of time playing video games, and in the summer, his family went on camping vacations. Bob's little sister was born shortly before Bob's parents bought him his first bike, and his little brother was born just after they bought him his second. As the family grew, they moved into a bigger house and spent a great deal of money on appliances, paint, tools, and other products. Bob himself will eventually grow up, start a family, and, like most Americans, live within a few miles of a Walmart store.

The bicycle category manager did a phenomenal job of putting together a product selection that appealed to Bob every time he was in the market for the kind of bikes that Walmart sells. However, if that is all Walmart sold to Bob's family, the company missed out on tens of thousands of dollars in sales. A customer manager might have realized that Bob would grow out of the bicycle category but would have worked hard to ensure that the company retained Bob (and his family) as a customer.

In the context of managing a chain of big-box stores, category management allows retailers to simplify the complexity of operating a store with thousands of individual SKUs. It also allows retailers to think beyond individual items to be more strategic about the role particular categories play and the tactics they use to attract and retain customers. However, the focus is still on the products rather than the customers. Ultimately, retailers should ensure that they have the right products for the customers they aim to serve, rather than looking for the right customers to buy the products they offer for sale.

This is not because retailers do not believe the customer comes first; it is because it was not practical to get to know individual customers' preferences until very recently. Historically, retailers were mostly constrained to think about their customer base in terms of aggregate sales statistics augmented by marketing research data. Target segments were large groups of customers with one thing in common – such as similar ages, life cycles, and/or geographical locations – and many differences. When retailers wanted to communicate with customers outside the store, they had few options beyond mass media broadcasts. Inside the store, customers shopped relatively anonymously, and companies did not know much about them.

Advanced analytics, supported by technology, have helped to change what consumer marketers are able to accomplish, but the point of those analytics is not data – it is a better understanding of the customer. Few have been more successful in implementing a system that focuses on the customer, under difficult economic conditions and in an intensely competitive industry, than Harrah's.

Betting on the Customer

Visitors walking down the strip in Las Vegas would find it hard not to be amazed by the spectacular developments and the intense focus on gaming and entertainment. Within a couple of blocks, visitors can travel through an Egyptian pyramid, New York City, Paris, Venice, and Rome. Inside these developments, world-class stage shows, restaurants, and nightclubs – and, of course, shopping – have become standard fare. On the street, hotels and casinos grab tourists' attention with roller coasters, dancing lakes, exploding volcanoes, and ship-to-ship pirate battles.

Nestled within all of the action and spectacle is Harrah's Las Vegas hotel and casino. Housed in a relatively uninteresting building without exceptional shows or restaurants, Harrah's seems out of place. Yet for the past decade, it has been widely regarded as the most successful gaming company on the continent. In 2005, Harrah's bought Caesar's Entertainment for just under $10 billion and became the world's largest casino entertainment company.[1] Today, the company is number one or two in market share in every major market in the United States. It owns and operates fifty-two casinos in seven countries on five continents, which includes approximately forty-two thousand hotel rooms and more than three million square feet of casino gaming space.[2] Moreover, it has accomplished this in a market in which customers make fewer trips to casinos and spend less per trip.[3]

So how did the company – which the *Wall Street Journal* once called "long a dowdy also-ran in the flashy casino business"[4] – become the dominant player in a hyper-competitive industry in a challenging economic climate? It bet on the customer.

While its competitors fell over each other to build the next big attraction, Harrah's bent over backward to serve its customers. Part of this is the philosophy of service that permeates the company, from the CEO to the valets who greet guests at the door and the maids who clean the rooms. But a BHAG, philosophy, mission, or vision is not enough. Most retailers say they focus on and care about customer service, but they fail to implement the systems and organizational structure to support that ideal.

Harrah's developed those systems and is a classic example of a company that subscribes to Peter Drucker's view that the primary purpose of a business is to acquire and keep customers. This may sound straightforward, but it stands in contrast to the more pervasive view that a corporation should, first and foremost, focus on maximizing shareholder value. The difference is that focusing on shareholder returns leads organizations to think in terms of cost reductions, financial controls, and labor productivity, rather than long-term growth in revenue and profitability.[5] Managing costs and increasing productivity are important to a business – however, they are not as important as acquiring and keeping customers. The problem is that when cost controls and employee productivity are an organization's chief concerns, the customer becomes secondary. As Gary Loveman, Caesar's former CEO, has argued, "Meeting the budget at the expense of service is a very bad idea. If you're not making your numbers, you don't cut back on staff."[6] Instead, Harrah's attributes its consistent growth in same-store sales to an absolute focus on customer satisfaction.

Of course, there are important caveats to this argument. First, in for-profit organizations, the commitment to customer satisfaction is a means to an end – that is, customer satisfaction is important because it drives revenue and profitability. In the extreme, if retailers ignored financial results, they could easily improve customer satisfaction by investing heavily in creating outstanding products and then simply giving those products away for free. Harrah's absolute focus on customer satisfaction means it invests heavily in understanding what truly drives satisfaction for each individual and then puts together a value proposition that appeals to that specific customer as cost-effectively as possible. That might mean managers are unable to meet their numbers in the short term. However, over the long term, Harrah's has created the most loyal customer base in the industry.

That loyalty sheltered the company against tough economic times and allowed it to grow while its competition struggled to survive. For example, after Harrah's implemented its focus on customer satisfaction at its casino in the very competitive market of Laughlin, Nevada, it grew its revenue by 14 percent year over year while the overall market grew by only 1 percent. As Harrah's invested in getting to know customers by name and understanding what they looked for from a casino – whether an occasional steak dinner, free play, or simply a friendly smile from an employee – its competitors built increasingly extravagant and expensive attractions in an attempt to add value to the customer experience. Harrah's realized the segment of consumers who wanted their casino to offer spectacular entertainment was over-served by competitors who constantly one-upped each other. At the same time, many other customers wanted a simpler gaming experience driven by personal service. When the company talks about an absolute focus on satisfying customers, it talks about customers it can profitably serve over the long term. The way Loveman saw it, he was happy to "let the neighbors lure tourists with knights on horseback, fiery volcanoes, pirate ships, and mini-Manhattans. We'll just keep refining what we're already pretty good at: drilling into our data and making sure our regular customers are more than satisfied."[7]

Second, if Harrah's alone had built an industry-leading business by focusing on customer satisfaction, its story would not be an important component of the retail value proposition. However, evidence to support business models that focus on acquiring and retaining customers has built steadily over the past couple of decades. Ironically for managers who believe shareholder value should be their paramount concern, study after study demonstrates that a customer-centric approach to management is the key to increasing shareholder value.[8] Investing in customer relationships has a powerful effect on stock prices because it drives revenue and profitability. In fact, research by Claes Fornell and colleagues has found that companies that invest in superior customer satisfaction are able to achieve the holy grail of higher returns with less risk.[9] It is not surprising, then, that retailers and researchers have turned their attention to better understanding the drivers of customer satisfaction.

Managing Customer Satisfaction: The Relationship Gap

Walgreens, the largest retail drugstore chain in the United States, started out as a small neighborhood store in Chicago. As legend has it, Charles R. Walgreen, Sr., enjoyed taking orders over the phone and, while chatting with a customer, would rush the delivery boy out the door. Walgreen would continue the conversation, getting to know his patron a little better, until he heard the customer's doorbell ring. Then, as the customer realized the delivery had arrived, Walgreen would exclaim, "Now *that* is customer service!" and hang up the phone.

Walgreen understood that the key to customer satisfaction is delivering an experience that exceeds expectations. The basic concept is fairly straightforward. A customer heads out to shop with some expectation of what the experience will be like. This expectation can include several of the elements of a retail value proposition that I have discussed throughout this book. For example, the customer might expect the store to have a convenient location, easy-to-navigate aisles, a good breadth of products to choose from, and reasonable prices. When the retailer exceeds these expectations – for example, if it is easier to get to the store than expected and the product selection is outstanding – customers tend to be more satisfied. When the retailer fails to meet them – for example, if the aisles are difficult to navigate or prices are surprisingly high – customers tend to be less satisfied. This is often referred to as the "gap" model of customer satisfaction, because what drives satisfaction is the gap – either positive or negative – between what customers expect and what they experience (figure 8.1).

For a retailer, this model comes back to understanding individual customers and their expectations. To a large extent, this is driven by what customers have previously experienced – that is, what the retailer and its competition have delivered in the past – as well as what they think the experience should be like. Market research, combined with a little competitive intelligence, can easily ascertain what customer baseline expectations are for a shopping experience in a particular category. Customer surveys and focus groups can also uncover details that consumers would like to be part of the experience but that no one has yet delivered. However, many major breakthroughs in retail are driven by ideas about products that customers do not yet know they want. For example, Starbucks was not created in response to a widespread demand for espresso drinks. Similarly, most consumers had no idea how important yoga clothing would be to their wardrobe before lululemon. Prior to Home Depot's launch of its warehouse-style home improvement stores, the industry assumed the concept was not viable, and most consumers were happy with the limited selection in smaller neighborhood stores.

That, of course, is part of the problem with constantly exceeding consumers' expectations: it is difficult to come up with the next great innovation on a regular basis. Relying on such innovations alone to drive customer satisfaction is a tenuous approach to competition over

Figure 8.1. The Gap Model of Customer Satisfaction

the long term for a retailer. Similarly, as ongoing market research and satisfaction surveys have become a staple of the retail and consumer marketing industries, it is difficult to uncover insights that the competition has not. In addition, even if a retailer is able to find an opportunity to improve customer satisfaction, once that insight is implemented, it is usually relatively easy for competitors to copy it. Finally, many organizations worry that any improvements to the current experience will only increase customer expectations on future shopping trips. As a result, whether through innovation or market research, it is extremely difficult to improve customer satisfaction over time by consistently exceeding expectations.

Fortunately, it is not necessary to do so.

Building Relationships

Think about the relationship between a retailer and a customer in terms of interpersonal relationships. The first time a consumer shops at a retail store she has not previously visited is a lot like a first date. If the experience is considerably worse than what the consumer expected, the probability of a "second date" is substantially lower. In contrast, if the first experience was much better than she expected, the probability of future dates is far higher. In general, during the first few shopping trips, the consumer more actively evaluates the new store relative to expectations. When the store fails to meet or exceed those expectations, it is likely to lose that consumer's business to a competitor. However, if it meets or exceeds expectations over the course of the first few visits, eventually a relationship between the consumer and the store develops (see figure 8.2).

As that relationship grows, the consumer moves from the state of active evaluation that characterizes initial shopping trips to a more habitual purchasing pattern. From the perspective of the interpersonal analogy, this is necessary for the survival of human relationships. Relationships would be very unstable if we all woke up every morning and objectively evaluated our partners and friends relative to "the competition." We are not wired to behave that way. It takes a lot of effort and energy for consumers to constantly search for information and evaluate all of the stores and alternatives they could consider before they make a purchase. People who are compelled to try to maximize the quality of the many decisions they make every day by fully considering all options tend to be very dissatisfied with their decisions and unhappy with their lives. Instead, most people tend to "satisfice"[10] and then rely on what worked for past decisions to inform future ones.[11] In other words, in a retail context, consumers tend to find a store they are satisfied with and then continue to shop there until that store no longer meets their needs.

Habit and the convenience that comes with familiarity drive many relationships between a retailer and a consumer. Store locations, interior designs and layouts, and product selections are very important in this regard to the extent that they facilitate convenience in routine shopping situations. For most consumers, traveling to a new store, navigating new aisles, and then finding desired products is not worth the effort.

Some relationships, however, go beyond habitual behavior and connect the consumer to the retailer in deeper and more meaningful ways. For example, consumers who are passionate about coffee, electronics, yoga, outdoor activities, or organic food may develop a strong relationship with their preferred provider of related products. Retailers such as Starbucks, Apple, lululemon, REI, and Whole Foods have been very

Figure 8.2. Relationships Built over Time through Retailer-Consumer Interaction

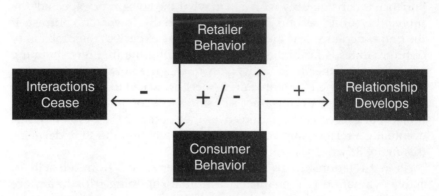

successful in this regard. The shopping experience for a segment of consumers in these types of retail stores is not just a routine purchase but part of who they are and a reflection of what they value. In addition to increasing the probability of repeat purchases, which habitual relationships also do, these more passionate relationships increase the likelihood that consumers will tell others about the retailer and become advocates for it.

Both habitual and passion-based relationships provide the retailer with several important benefits that are difficult to obtain in any other way. Ultimately, when managed well, each of these relationship benefits can translate into improved revenue and profitability over the long term.

EFFICIENCY

Shoppers who are more familiar with a retailer are able to shop more efficiently and with less support. This increases the dollars spent per second shopping and reduces the costs of service. Consumers who value their time are better off when they can complete a shopping trip more efficiently. On its own, improved shopping efficiency is a substantial relationship benefit for both the consumer and the retailer.

ACCOMMODATION

Consumers who feel strongly connected to one retailer relative to its competition are willing to make more of an effort to accommodate that retailer. For example, a consumer passionate about the Caribou Coffee experience is more likely to drive past a Starbucks to get to a Caribou café than a consumer who considers the two stores to be more or less equivalent. Similarly, a retail-banking client who has a long-term relationship with Wells Fargo is more likely to accommodate the bank's hours of operation and less likely to be tempted away if another bank offers longer hours. This type of accommodation has tangible benefits for the retailer, such as a larger trading area for each of its stores as customers are willing to travel farther. In addition, when its customers are more accommodating, a retailer can thrive with fewer locations and shorter hours, which reduces overall costs of operation. It may even be able to get away with a limited selection of brands within its product line. Companies such as Apple and IKEA have benefited from this type of relationship with customers.

TOLERANCE AND FORGIVENESS

Every company makes mistakes and fails to adequately serve some of its customers at some point. If those failures happen during the initial points of contact between a retailer and its customers, it is increasingly difficult and expensive to attract those dissatisfied customers back to the store. However, solid customer relationships can help protect the retailer against those times when it does not meet consumers' expectations. For example, the consumer who has habitually bought milk from the same grocery store for years will forgive the retailer the one time milk is out of stock. While a customer visiting that grocery store for the first time might see a milk stock-out as a sign of poor management, the regular customer knows it is an unusual occurrence and is much less likely to attribute the failure to a general lack of quality in the store. In fact, the stronger the relationship is, the more likely it is that consumers will forgive even major service failures. For example, many Toyota customers continued to believe the company made the highest-quality cars and trucks, even after a high-profile failure resulted in Toyota's being called before Congress.[12] To a large extent, this tolerance is based on a long history of exceeding the expectations of customers who have become passionate about the products. A strong relationship with consumers can give the retailer the benefit of the doubt when an experience does not meet expectations.

PERCEPTUAL BIAS

Just as we tend to see our close friends and family differently than we do strangers, consumers tend to perceive retailers with which they have a relationship differently from those with which they do not. This can be especially important when it is difficult to accurately and objectively assess key decision criteria such as product quality or price competitiveness. The most striking example of this type of bias comes from the power of the Coke brand during taste tests. In blind tests, Coke regularly loses out to Pepsi. Even some regular Coke drinkers who say they have a strong preference for Coke over Pepsi choose Pepsi when the taste test is blind. However, when the taste test is not blind, Coke wins regularly. Clearly, at least some of the consumers who prefer Coke are biased when they assess their preference for the brand. This type of perceptual bias is not necessarily a conscious response – that is, Coke drinkers do not see the label and pretend to enjoy Coke more even though Pepsi tastes better. Instead, they respond differently to the taste when they know it is Coke rather than just a cola. This type of bias can develop through habitual consumption as consumers become familiar and comfortable with a brand, as well as through a passionate connection to one retailer over others. In many categories – from produce to sweaters to tires to cosmetics – it is very difficult to objectively say which products are the best. In these markets, strong consumer relationships can play an important role in establishing a perceptual advantage.

Of course, this is true in other areas as well. For example, which grocery retailer offers the lowest prices? Some shoppers argue the answer is Costco, while others are equally sure it is Walmart. Other customers might argue that when sales and Kroger rewards are taken into account, Kroger offers the least expensive grocery basket. Given that retailers constantly adjust prices and product selections, it is difficult, if not impossible, to definitively know who offers the lowest prices on a particular basket of goods at any one time. In general, loyal customers tend to evaluate the retailers they patronize and the brands they buy more favorably on price, quality, and other attributes than non-loyal consumers.[13] This bias is created over time as a relationship develops through positive interactions that meet or exceed consumers' expectations. However, such a relationship is not impervious to reality, and that same favoritism can be lost over time if the retailer consistently fails to meet expectations.

TRUST

Trust is a central component of strong relationships and, like the relationship itself, takes time to build. Nevertheless, in a world of increasing complexity and an often overwhelming array of choices for consumers, trust may be the most important currency in retailing.

Many of the critical parts of the retailing process break down without trust. Whether in product safety, quality, corporate social responsibility, fair pricing, or several other key factors in customers' choices, without trust sales suffer. To earn this trust, retailers need to consistently deliver on their promises and perform at a level that is equivalent to, if not better than, that of the competition.

Consumers would like to trust the companies that they interact with but have learned to be wary of offers that appear too good to be true, high-pressure sales tactics, and low-quality products. Given the high-profile cases regarding lead in toys, listeriosis in meat, automobile and pharmaceutical recalls, poor environmental or social records, and general lack of performance that meets expectations, people are rightfully guarded in their retail spending. Yet, it is very expensive in terms of time and effort for consumers to review product information and corporate performance extensively before making their purchases. Especially for the many routine purchases consumers make on a daily or weekly basis – such as groceries, gasoline, apparel, pharmaceuticals, home improvement items, and so on – being able to trust that a retailer behaves in a fair and ethical manner can greatly simplify consumers' lives. From the retailer's perspective, having customers' trust means less money spent on advertising, less need to discount prices, easier new product introductions, greater loyalty, and a potent barrier to competition.

ADVOCACY

Finally, great relationships lead consumers to recommend the retailer to their friends and family. When customers are excited by and engaged in the shopping experience, they want to talk about it. This can range from finding jeans that fit perfectly to getting great advice on a home renovation project to experiencing a new in-store environment (e.g., a climbing wall at REI or the Cars repair shop at the Disney Store).

Advocacy, however, is difficult to achieve. In many cases, a retailer may exceed expectations and build a relationship that leads to customer loyalty without advocacy. It helps if the consumer is passionate about the product category and likely to discuss it with friends. Automobile enthusiasts might talk about a recent or planned car purchase. Fashionistas tend to talk about the clothes they buy and where they buy them. Foodies are more apt to talk about a restaurant or grocery shopping experience.

Similarly, a surprising or unusual experience is more likely to generate a Facebook post or a cocktail party conversation. Virgin has successfully created this kind of word of mouth through CEO Richard Branson's publicity stunts and celebrity status. Other retail companies have used pop-up stores or short-term events to draw attention and start conversations. For example, when MAC Cosmetics opened a temporary or "pop-up" shop in Rome, it received global media coverage. The Generic Man opened up a store for one month in a Los Angeles Urban Outfitters, and Reebok opened a one-month store named FLASH in New York City's CVZ contemporary art gallery. Year after year, Apple uses secretive new product launches to keep people guessing and talking about what it will do next.

Retailers that are clearly differentiated from the competition generate advocacy. In its early days, Starbucks grew this way by selling a style of coffee that was novel to most North Americans at a price many times that of the competition. Having experienced something so different and unexpected, consumers were eager to tell others about the encounter. Similarly, lululemon offered such a distinctive style of active wear that it inspired customers to spread the word about its innovative products. Of course, not all retailers are able to create word of mouth through a revolutionary product introduction. Fortunately, they do not need to. Retailers can also create unique service experiences that stand out in the consumer's mind. Jill's Table, a home and giftware store in London, Ontario, has developed a very loyal base of customer advocates through exceptional service and customer care.[14] Owner Jill Wilcox and her employees make an effort to get to know individual customers by name. On occasion, during the hectic holiday season, they stand curbside in the snow to complete a drive-by handoff of a desired product to a customer too busy to park and enter the store. Jill's Table also offers skillets to unsure gourmets to try out at home before they make a purchase. Importantly, these are not premeditated marketing gimmicks. They are the result of the passion the staff have for serving their customers.

The Importance of Employee Engagement

As much as consumers are willing to enter into a relationship with a retailer because of a great environment or product selection or customer service, the best relationships are not between customers and buildings or products or procedures. They are between people: customers and employees. Strong internal systems, processes, procedures, and training can facilitate customer satisfaction driven by great service, but at the end of the day those systems fail without employees who are willing and even excited to serve customers. What distinguishes Jill's Table from its competitors is not the products or location but the interactions between staff and customers.

Unfortunately, most employees are not engaged in their work and, as a result, do not engage customers. Since the 1970s, Gallup has polled workers to measure such engagement. The survey results indicate that for the average company in North America, only one in three employees is engaged in his work. About half of employees surveyed are not engaged, and just under 20 percent are actively disengaged – that is, almost one employee in every five is working against the interests of his employer. These employees not only directly hurt the organization's earnings; they also interfere with the work of other staff members and deflate morale. According to Gallup, actively disengaged employees cost more than $300 billion in lost productivity in the United States.[15] Building on these results, Gallup reanalyzed its data from 199 studies including 152 independent organizations from dozens of countries around the world. As that meta-analysis clearly indicates, companies that are better at engaging employees have more loyal customers, superior profitability, greater productivity, and less shrinkage.[16] For retailers that want to improve customer satisfaction and benefit from stronger customer relationships, the message is clear: engaged employees are the key to engaged customers and, ultimately, improved shareholder value.

Chapter Nine

Customer Valuation

During the fall of 2006, Sears Canada introduced an innovative customer service initiative across its chain of full-line Canadian department stores: the services of a shopping "Elf." The Elves, Sears' version of a personal shopper, were selected from among the most engaged and productive store sales associates. On average, a Sears store had approximately seven to ten Elves who received special training to allow them to better connect with customers, build relationships, and improve Sears' business performance. Personal shoppers were not new to Canadian department stores, but traditionally they were available only in higher-priced retailers.

Customers could pre-book an Elf, or connect with one at the in-store "Wish Station." The Elves were knowledgeable associates who could help customers find products, make recommendations, and potentially cross-sell products between different departments. Sears believed the Elves would make a substantial contribution to the retailer's ability to exceed customers' expectations and build relationships, which could create a competitive advantage. Sears carefully integrated the program with its more general segmentation scheme and aimed to improve the relationship with those customers who tended to visit the store primarily to buy gifts during the holiday season. The Elf program was designed to make gift buying easier and more enjoyable, especially among time-starved holiday shoppers. Sears also selected a series of metrics by which to measure the performance of individual Elves and the Elf program as a whole. These included sales per square foot, sales per hour per associate, traffic count, number of transactions, and average transaction size.

In essence, the Elf program was Sears' attempt to move away from a focus on products toward a focus on customers and their purchasing behavior across a wider range of product categories. It was an interesting and innovative approach to improving customer service in the department store industry, which for years had suffered from a reputation for declining service quality. Unfortunately for Sears and its customers, the program failed to flourish and was soon scaled back and eventually discontinued. Sears, like many other retailers before it, realized that although satisfaction is important, when spending money to improve customer relationships, the results need to be justified by a sufficient return on the investment. For retail managers this should raise two important questions. First, how do retailers measure the return on investments in satisfaction? And, second, where should retailers spend the available resources to get the maximum bang for a buck? The answer is by focusing on the *right* customers and, counter-intuitively, acknowledging that not all customers are right.

Not All Customers Are Right

As I discussed in the previous chapter, many retail executives continue to manage their business as if profits come exclusively from the design of the shopping environment or the management of product assortments. In reality, of course, profits come from customers – the people who buy those products in those shopping environments. However, not all customers are profitable. In fact, most merchants will tell you their business is really driven by something akin to the retail version of the Pareto Principle – that is, 80 percent of the company's profits come from 20 percent of its customers.

In *Angel Customers & Demon Customers*, Larry Selden and Geoffrey Colvin make a stronger and (for many readers) more disturbing claim. Specifically, their research suggests that retailers would be more accurate to think in terms of a 150–20 rule, whereby the top 20 percent of the company's customers generate 150 percent of its profits, while the bottom 20 percent of customers cost the company 150 percent of its profits. As a result, the 60 percent in the middle determine if and to what extent the company will make money. The authors call the top 20 percent angel customers and the bottom 20 percent demon customers. While at some level all successful businesses are aware of the importance of their best customers, Selden and Colvin highlight the fact that the bottom 20 percent are equally important – but their effect is in the opposite direction.

To many, the idea that a large proportion of a retailer's customers cost money is initially counter-intuitive. After all, when a customer buys an appropriately priced product, the retailer makes a profit, right? The answer would be "yes" if every product price was based on the cost of completing that particular sale. In practice, retailers tend to choose one price at which they offer a specific product for sale at any given time. I will get into the intricacies of pricing in chapter 11, but for now it is reasonable to assume that prices are usually set to ensure that a profit is made on the average sale. The problem with this approach is that it does not take into account the different costs of selling to different customers.

For example, some customers walk into a store during normal operating hours, find the products they wish to purchase, pick up a couple of unplanned items, and pay at a self-checkout kiosk. The cost of selling a product to that customer is relatively small and so the profitability of that customer is high. Other customers buy in ways that reduce or even eliminate the true profit the retailer is able to realize. For example, the customer who purchases products only when they are on sale can help a retailer increase overall sales volume and inventory turnover, but each transaction with such a customer is less profitable than a sale to someone who is less price sensitive. As I discussed in chapter 4, consumers who only make planned purchases are of less value to the company. Similarly, consumers who require a lot of assistance and return products cost more in staff time than those who shop more independently and keep what they buy. Customers who shop at odd hours require the store to pay more in overhead and staff to stay open longer. Along the same lines, when a retailer devotes shelf space to unpopular products, it gives up space it could use to promote better-selling items. Retailers are happy to accommodate people who engage in some of these behaviors. That is simply the cost of doing business with a variety of consumer segments that have different preferences. However, when all the expenses of the sale are taken into account, consumers who engage in multiple costly behaviors can eat up the profit margin built into the price and, in some cases, can end up costing the company significant amounts of money. These customers are the "demons" Selden and Colvin refer to when they say 20 percent of customers cost the company 150 percent of its profits.

Recognizing the existence of both angel and demon customers leads retailers to a different perspective on customer management. Specifically, it makes sense to pursue the approaches discussed in this book to design shopping environments and create compelling product selections to engage angel customers – but not demons. In fact, losing a demon customer impacts financial performance approximately as much as gaining or retaining an angel customer. Similarly, turning a customer from the middle 60 percent into an angel, or preventing that customer from becoming a demon, can substantially improve profitability. From this perspective, firing the wrong customers is as critical to retail success as acquiring the right ones. To do either well requires a reliable means of sorting the demons from the angels.

One Question Is Not Enough

A very popular approach to segmenting customers based on their value and the relationship they have with the retailer is the net-promoter score.[1] A wide variety of organizations that sell to consumers – ranging from banks to department stores to airlines – use this score extensively. The appeal of the net-promoter score is its simplicity and directness. It is based on only one question: "How likely is it that you would recommend our company to a friend or colleague?"

Consumers respond to this question on an eleven-point scale, where zero is not at all likely, five is neutral, and ten is extremely likely. The score is then computed by segmenting respondents into three groups. The first group is composed of those who responded with a nine or ten; they are the valuable "promoter" customers who are the most likely to refer other valuable customers to the company. The second group includes moderately satisfied customers who responded with a rating of seven or eight. The third group is composed of those who responded with a rating between zero and six. These consumers are labeled "detractors" and are somewhat akin to Selden and Colvin's demons. Detractors are not engaged and may in fact actively harm the relationships that other, more valuable customers have with the retailer. To calculate the net-promoter score, the percentage of detractors is subtracted from the percentage of promoters.[2] Companies with negative scores should be concerned about the relationship they have with their customers. Consumer-centric organizations should expect to have a positive score – that is, more promoters than detractors in their customer base. A score above 20 percent is generally considered to signal an above-average level of customer engagement.

Overall, this is about as effective a measure as an organization can get from a single question. It is simple to collect and straightforward to analyze, which means it can be a relatively cost-effective and efficient way to gauge general sentiment within a retailer's customer base. In addition, a retailer can ask the same question about its competitors, which creates a standardized metric for comparison.

The problem is that it is only one question. As more than one organization has realized, a sudden increase or decrease in this score is difficult to explain or act on based on a single score on an eleven-point scale. The question does not capture any direct information about important aspects of the consumer decision process, including perceptions of quality, value, or even satisfaction. It is simply a self-reported measure of how likely consumers are to refer the company to others. That is a valuable insight into the relationship between a retailer and a customer, but on its own it is insufficient. Moreover, subsequent to the initial publication and broad adoption of the net-promoter score, follow-up research indicated that it is, in fact, not a great predictor of actual consumer behavior.[3] To truly understand the value of a customer base, it is important to build models that include data beyond what can be collected by any one question.

RFM Models

Economists, psychologists, and market researchers have long believed that one of the best ways to predict future behavior is to look at past behavior. In other words, if you want to know how likely a customer is to shop at a retailer, how soon they will return, and how much they will spend, it is helpful to know how often they have shopped at the store in the past, how recently they visited the store, and how much they usually spend. This perspective has led retailers to begin to think of customer value in terms of recency, frequency, and monetary spend (RFM) variables.

Consider, for example, Barnes and Noble's (B&N) Membership program. This loyalty program is designed to give high-purchase-volume customers a better price on the books they buy. Customers who are members pay an upfront annual fee and then receive discounts that range from 40 percent off bestsellers to 10 percent off books purchased online, plus free shipping for online orders.[4] A customer who buys enough books during the year earns back the upfront annual fee and starts to save on his overall annual purchases. In return for these discounts, B&N collects RFM customer data – that is, it knows when the last purchase was made (recency), how often the customer makes a purchase at any store or online (frequency), and how much the customer spends in a year (monetary).

When using an RFM model, the retailer may decide to look back at prior years' data to see how important each of the RFM variables are in predicting the profitability of individual program members. If the company finds the amount customers spent in the previous year explains 50 percent of the amount they spent in the subsequent year, it might decide to give a 50 percent weight to the monetary variable in the current data to predict the value of its customers in the year to come. Following the same logic, B&N might apply a 30 percent weight to frequency and a 20 percent weight to recency. In addition, the company will have to decide how to standardize each variable – that is, choose a method of converting R, F, and M measures into a common scale – and then use those new weighted variables to generate a score for each customer. The added complexity and cost of RFM models can make the one-question net-promoter score look attractive. However, retailers that use more sophisticated measures – by either building the in-house expertise or outsourcing the analytical details to a specialist firm – are able to improve the accuracy with which they value their customer base.

With this type of RFM model, a retailer such as B&N can use the assigned scores to sort and rank individual customers to create value-based segments. The retailer can then use this information to focus resources in a way that maximizes the probability of a solid return on investment. For example, B&N could spend more money to retain and even increase the amount the most valuable customers spend, and could curtail or even eliminate marketing to the least valuable customers. The retailer could also combine what it learns from its RFM model with other segmentation schemes based on geographic or demographic information. This would provide some insight into which customers have the potential to be more valuable and possibly highlight those people who may be valuable prospects but are not yet customers – because they live in neighborhoods or belong to demographic groups that tend to spend more on the types of products a company like Barnes and Noble sells. Finally, using product preference information – for example, fiction, non-fiction, business books, children's books, and so on – a retailer could further refine marketing programs to reach the right customers with a relevant message.

Customer Lifetime Value

RFM models based on past behavior are popular because the requisite data are relatively easy to collect, and research indicates that these variables have a reasonable ability to predict future behavior.[5] However, although past behavior is a good predictor, it is still an imperfect indicator of the ideal measurement – that is, the future value of a customer to the business. The focus of RFM is on what has happened in the past, given the conditions that existed – such as the competitive environment, economic climate, product innovations, and so on. Those variables do not take into account how the ongoing evolution of the retail marketplace has affected what customers currently think. Therefore, retailers would really like to understand past behavior and incorporate some insight into the current psychographic characteristics of the consumer, such as consumers' perceptions of quality and value, customer satisfaction, depth of customer relationships, and the likelihood of referral.

In addition, RFM models are usually designed to predict behavior in only the next period (e.g., the following quarter or year) and, as a result, are primarily applicable to short-term managerial decisions. They also tend to focus more on revenue, with limited or no accounting for the costs generating that revenue. As I discussed earlier in this book, as important as revenue is, retailers are ultimately interested in profitability, which requires incorporating costs into models of customer value. This has led some retailers to begin to assess customers in terms of their lifetime value, integrating information about profit margins, acquisition costs, and retention rates into predictive models. Formally, customer lifetime value (CLV) is estimated using an equation along the following lines:

$$CLV = (M / (1 - r + i)) - AC$$

In this equation, M is the profit margin, r is the retention rate (and $1 - r$ is the rate at which customers are being lost), i is the cost of capital (e.g., the rate of interest the company has to pay on money it borrows), and AC is the cost of acquiring a customer. Essentially, this formula is designed to capture the profitability (M) of a customer over the expected lifetime of that customer ($1 - r + i$), while taking into account what it cost to acquire that customer in the first place (AC).

Thinking about customers in this way changes the focus from ensuring that each individual transaction is profitable to considering the total profitability of a customer over his lifetime. A potential implication of this approach is that it makes sense for a retailer to spend a significant amount of money during the initial transactions to build a strong relationship (i.e., *AC*, the acquisition cost), even if it means that during the first few months of that relationship the retailer loses money, because in the long run that customer will generate substantial profits. It also highlights the importance of retaining current customers (*r*), because the lower the probability that the customer will be retained over the long term, the less sense it makes to invest in acquiring that customer in the first place (or the higher the profit margins have to be). Thinking in terms of customer lifetime value is about focusing on customers' potential return on investment.

Of course, the more precise the inputs into the equation – that is, the more accurately a retailer calculates profit margins and acquisition costs – the more exact the ultimate estimate of customer value will be. Nevertheless, even simplified calculations can capture the spirit of the CLV metric and provide important data that can inform the customer-focused manager's decisions. For example, imagine that an ice cream shop is considering buying a new machine that can dispense ice cream cones much faster than its current hand-scooped process. As a result, staff would be able to serve more customers every hour and reduce the time that customers spend in line during periods of peak demand. The store manager knows waiting in line reduces customer satisfaction, but is not sure if the machine is worth the investment. The machine itself costs just under $10,000 and comes with a maintenance plan that guarantees the store will not have to pay for upkeep for the next seven years.

From a simple product sales perspective, it will take a lot of additional ice cream cones for the store to break even. The manager, however, is thinking about the problem in terms of customer value rather than product sales. In a recent satisfaction survey of the store's loyalty card members, the manager found two different satisfaction segments. Although overall his loyalty card members were satisfied with their in-store experience, some were happier than others. He categorized one group as "moderately satisfied" and the other as "highly satisfied." Connecting the data from loyalty card transactions to the survey results, he knew the average number of visits each group made per week and the average profit the store received from each visit. Prior research told him that highly satisfied customers tended to continue to patronize the company a lot longer than those who were only moderately satisfied. At the same time, even highly satisfied customers did not remain customers forever – they moved to new neighborhoods, their kids grew up and stopped eating ice cream, or they switched to a competitor. With this information, he calculated the profitability of these two segments of customers and estimated the lifetime value of each group (see table 9.1).

At an average profitability on all sales (including loyalty card and the less profitable non-loyalty card customers) of about seventy-five cents, the ice cream shop would have to sell more than thirteen thousand additional ice cream cones to break even. However, the information in table 9.1 provides a different perspective. Converting a moderately satisfied customer into a highly satisfied customer results in an additional annual profit of about $52 and an additional lifetime profit of $381. Therefore, to break even, the new ice cream machine would have to speed up service enough to move twenty-six customers from moderately to highly satisfied. The manager realized that this was a rough calculation and that retail is an inherently risky business that makes predicting the future difficult, but taking a CLV approach gave him the information he needed to confidently invest in the new ice cream machine.

As with RFM models, CLV calculations can be integrated with other information, such as geographic, demographic, and product preference data. In addition, more sophisticated CLV models can incorporate consumers' responses to surveys that measure important psychographic information, such as customer satisfaction, perceptions of product value, and brand relationships. For example, Roland Rust and colleagues have developed a survey that estimates customer lifetime value and incorporates both past behavior and current psychographic information.[6] This type of approach can provide insight into the value of individual customers. In addition, when the value of each individual customer is added up across the entire business to create a measure of overall *customer equity*, the retailer has a powerful metric to assess the future value of its entire customer base. Understanding the value of the customers served provides important information to retail managers as they decide where to focus resources and how to craft their retail value proposition.

As a whole, retail is quickly becoming a field that requires managers and executives to be skilled in quantitative models and decisions that incorporate increasingly sophisticated analytics. At the end of the day, however, the goal is not to develop the most mathematically complex models but to better understand the value of a retailer's customer base.

Table 9.1 Customer Lifetime Value – The Ice Cream Shop Example

	Moderately Satisfied	Highly Satisfied
Visits per week	0.8	1.5
Visits per year	41.6	78
Profit per visit	$0.80	$1.10
Profit per year	$33.28	$85.80
Average customer lifetime	2.2	5.3
Profit per lifetime	$73.22	$454.74

For some, using simple measures such as the net-promoter score is a good first step. Others look for a competitive advantage in increasingly refined and accurate quantitative predictions of the future value of individual consumers. For all retailers, it is clearly important to develop a method to separate the angels and demons within the customer base. Doing so improves the return on investment in marketing, merchandising, human resources, shopping environment design, product assortment management, and other critical areas.

Dealing with Demons

This book is about building a unique value proposition that attracts targeted customer segments. However, the research on customer valuation indicates that retailers also need to have a strategy for managing consumers who have a negative impact on the firm's performance – demons and detractors. At a general level, there are four different ways to approach this problem. I have discussed the first in detail already – that is, developing a method for valuing customers and focusing on those that have the best potential for a solid return on investment. Second, retailers can work to minimize the service failures and negative critical incidents that turn otherwise reasonable customers into demons. Similarly, businesses need to have a plan to deal with catastrophic critical incidents – ranging from contaminated products to severe service failures – that can dramatically change public perceptions and potentially cause irreversible damage to a brand. Third, retailers need to have a plan to deal with detractors – that is, an outline of the process of responding to or managing the fallout from customers who generate negative word of mouth about the company. Fourth, and most importantly, retailers must be proactive in the way they treat their customers and interact with their communities to build the relationships that can help to insulate them against the service failures and negative critical incidents that inevitably arise in retailing.

Managing Negative Critical Incidents

Regardless of the sophistication of quality management and employee training systems, sooner or later retailers fail to serve their customers as effectively as they would like. The cause can be as simple as an employee who is having a bad day or as complex as a breakdown in the global supply chain. Nevertheless, at some point retail managers face failures that create unhappy customers. These *negative critical incidents* are one of the great opportunities for creating a competitive advantage in contemporary retailing.

The idea that failure leads to a competitive advantage may initially sound counter-intuitive, but think of it from the customer's perspective. In a world where all retailers work hard to satisfy customers, it is difficult for any individual retailer to truly differentiate itself on satisfaction alone. For example, today many shoppers say they are happy with the service they receive at Kroger, Whole Foods, and Costco. As a result, the next time they go shopping, they will not be able to choose a grocer based on how satisfied they are with the retail experience. Dissatisfaction, on the other hand, is increasingly important. If a customer is satisfied with the experience at Kroger and Whole Foods but recently had a negative experience at Costco, then it is likely that the negative experience will play a critical role in future store choices.

In addition, the Internet and, in particular, online social networking have accelerated and amplified word of mouth. Historically, an upset consumer may have told a handful of friends about an outstanding or an upsetting experience at a local store. Today, consumers can effortlessly tell hundreds of friends about what they like and dislike. Consumers can gush about an exciting new product or a fantastic service experience in seconds by posting on Facebook or Twitter. Similarly, when a retail experience fails to meet their expectations, consumers need only a few keystrokes to tweet or post a negative message to hundreds of people, who can then easily pass that message on to hundreds more. As a result, service successes and failures that used to be between a store and a customer are now between the store, the customer, and the customer's extended social network.

The good news is that the strongest relationships are those that experience the inevitable ups and downs of human interaction. From the retailer's perspective, a service failure is a potential opportunity to demonstrate that the company values the customer's business by responding quickly and compassionately to the problem. In other words, retailers need to have an effective strategy for dealing with negative critical incidents. Moreover, as with other consumer-centric retail strategies, the retailer should tailor the response to negative critical incidents to the needs of specific customer segments.

Given the growing importance of this topic, researchers have started to investigate the best ways to respond to negative critical incidents on a segment-by-segment basis. For example, recent work by researchers such as Jenny van Doorn and Peter Verhoef has provided a starting point for thinking about how to manage service failures in terms of customer satisfaction and market share.[7] Specifically, this work pushes businesses to think in terms of how well they have met or exceeded customers' expectations in the past and what percentage of the market currently buys from them.

Adapted from van Doorn and Verhoef,[8] the *relationship management matrix* outlined in figure 9.1 is one example of how companies can address negative critical incidents within a customer base segmented by satisfaction and market share. The segment the company is performing most poorly in is the bottom left quadrant. Here, customer satisfaction is low and the company serves a small portion of the overall market. The company has not met the expectations of these customers, and any additional negative critical incidents are likely to continue to poison the relationship. Not surprisingly, the retailer cannot afford to disappoint these customers again and should focus on avoiding any further failures.

However, the problem of service failures is less dire in the remaining three segments. When a company has a large market share of less satisfied customers (the bottom right quadrant of figure 9.1), it likely has more time and opportunity to address problems as they arise. The fact that customers are not highly satisfied suggests that the firm has some other advantage that compensates for failing to meet consumers' expectations. Airlines, banks, and telecommunications companies, for example, often have a segment of customers who are not highly satisfied but continue to patronize the business because of lack of differentiated competition, contracts, or other barriers to switching. Eventually, an innovative competitor is likely to acquire those dissatisfied consumers,

Figure 9.1. Strategic Responses to Negative Critical Incidents

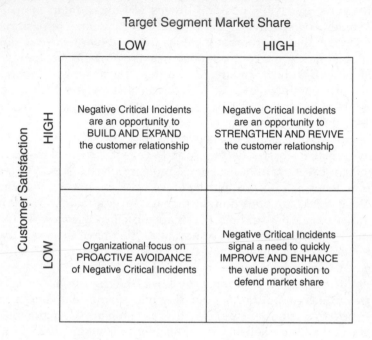

Target Segment Market Share

but in the short term the company has time to improve its offering to better meet expectations.

One of the most interesting results of research in this area is that among a retailer's most satisfied customers, a negative critical incident should be viewed as an opportunity to build and strengthen the relationship. In other words, not only are critical incidents survivable, they are a real opportunity to improve the value of a retailer's customer base. Most of the interactions between consumers and retailers are habitual and routine. Customers primarily focus on shopping efficiently and give very little thought or attention to the relationship they have with the company. However, when the company fails to meet expectations, that relationship comes into question. The customer who took her satisfaction with the retailer for granted suddenly questions the value she receives for her money. Yet, because her prior interactions were positive, the consumer is likely to give the retailer the benefit of the doubt. When the retailer responds effectively, the customer is again satisfied and soon falls back into a comfortable pattern of consumption, feeling even more confident in the relationship.

For example, consider a consumer who buys a new PlayStation on-line at Sony.com. The console is shipped to his home; he sets it up and begins to play with it that evening. After an hour or so, the console breaks. Now the consumer is frustrated because his new console has failed. In addition, he knows that when his kids wake up tomorrow morning they will be pretty upset that he broke the PlayStation before they had a chance to use it. The consumer had not really thought about his relationship with Sony before the console broke, but now he is intensely focused on it. He realizes that over the years he has purchased several different electronics from Sony, including a couple of televisions, a computer, a stereo system, and his favorite headphones. As per the instructions on Sony's website, he packages the PlayStation up and sends it back to the company to be repaired. He is not sure what will happen next. Will the company blame him and force him to buy another console? Will they take weeks to repair it? He has already begun to reconsider his choice of the PlayStation and regret not purchasing Microsoft's Xbox. Ultimately, he decides to give Sony a week to solve the problem. If they have not dealt with it by then, he plans to boycott the brand and spend his consumer electronics dollars elsewhere.

For Sony, this customer has a high lifetime value because he has loyally purchased the company's products for years. He has not been particularly price sensitive and has happily recommended Sony products to friends and family. That relationship is now at a critical point. If Sony sends a new or repaired PlayStation to the customer in a couple of days with an apology and a discount on his next game purchase, it can create an advocate and retain an angel customer. If the company blames the customer, claims the repair is not covered under the product's warranty, or returns the product too slowly, it risks losing this customer's future business. On one hand, if the company focuses only on the PlayStation sale, it might not make sense to quickly ship a new console out to the customer. That effort is likely to eliminate most of the profit from the transaction. On the other hand, from a customer lifetime value perspective, failing to adequately deal with this critical incident puts future profits at risk. For a company the size of Sony, this one customer is not going to make any real difference to financial performance. However, not having systems in place to identify this type of negative critical incident means that the company is likely to disappoint tens of thousands of customers who experience this and other types of service failures. As a result, it will lose many angel customers and create a new army of demons – the overall effect of which can be devastating to a retailer's financial performance. Therefore, rather than looking at negative critical incidents as simply something to avoid, it is important for retailers to have a plan to deal with service failures when they occur. Doing so allows a company to build and expand relationships where it has a relatively small market share and strengthen and revive relationships where it has a relatively large market share.

In addition to having a plan to deal with service failures that occur on a regular basis, organizations are finding it increasingly important to have a plan to deal with less likely – but more potentially damaging – catastrophic critical incidents (CCIs). Many successful companies have been forced to deal with CCIs in recent years. The classic example may be the 1982 Tylenol recall – often referred to as "the Chicago Tylenol murders" – after an unknown suspect tampered with the product and killed seven people. Although Johnson & Johnson was not at fault, it quickly and transparently addressed the issue and improved product packaging to reduce the risk of a repeat incident. A more recent list of CCIs includes the following: in 2007, tests discovered lead paint in Thomas the Tank Engine toys; in 2008, listeria contaminated Maple Leaf Foods' meat products, which resulted in several consumer deaths; in 2009, an acceleration problem in Toyota automobiles resulted in recalls and U.S. Congressional hearings; in 2010, oil spilled into the Gulf of Mexico from British Petroleum's Deepwater Horizon platform; in 2013, lululemon upset customers with sheer yoga pants; in 2014, Dov Charney, the founder and CEO of American Apparel, was fired after a decade of sexual harassment charges; and in 2015, Chrysler recalled 1.4 million vehicles after hackers demonstrated they could take control of a Jeep over the Internet. In fact, major product problems and costly recalls happen on a regular basis.

An interesting case study in the contrast between Michael McCain's handling of the 2008 listeriosis crisis at Maple Leaf Foods and Tony Hayward's handling of the 2010 BP oil spill highlights the importance of being prepared to deal with CCIs that seem unthinkable before they happen. While McCain was widely lauded for his honesty and transparency in addressing the food crisis that put century-old Maple Leaf Foods at risk, Hayward was fired for his public comments suggesting that the oil spill was a minor incident and a personal inconvenience to him. CCIs are by definition large-scale catastrophic events that are unlikely to occur and close to impossible to predict. In general, companies with strong customer relationships and a well-thought-out and well-executed plan have survived CCIs, while others have made bad situations worse.

Managing the Satisfaction Distribution

In the mid-1990s, Jeremy Dorosin purchased two espresso machines – one as a wedding gift and one for himself – from Starbucks. He had problems with both machines. Over a series of interactions, Starbucks and Dorosin failed to reach an amicable solution to the dispute. At one point Dorosin demanded that Starbucks replace the $189 machine he had bought as a wedding gift for $189 with a $2,500 one. Starbucks eventually sent a full refund to Dorosin along with a letter of apology, both of which he rejected.[9]

Shortly after the initial dispute, Dorosin spent tens of thousands of dollars on ads in the *Wall Street Journal* asking if other consumers had had similar experiences. He later created a website, Starbucked.com, to complain about the way he had been treated and to compile complaints from others about the company. He has been an active crusader against Starbucks for almost two decades.

In retrospect, some might think Starbucks should have simply given Dorosin the top-of-the-line machines and saved themselves the headache of dealing with such a determined detractor. Of course, retail businesses that regularly deal with thousands, or in this case millions, of customers around the world cannot give away hundreds of dollars to every dissatisfied customer. Just as some customers feel an irrational love for a retailer, others feel disproportionate hate. It just is not possible to make everyone happy all of the time. Instead, retailers should aim to manage the distribution of satisfaction within their customer base (see figure 9.2). That means there will always be demon consumers who have a negative effect on the business in one tail of the distribution.

As I have discussed in this chapter, as far as possible retailers want to minimize the percentage of their customer base that falls into the demon category. Conversely, the other end of the tail has angel customers who together drive growth, profitability, and ultimately shareholder value for the organization. The more of these customers a company has, the better off it is. In the middle of the distribution are the typical customers who like the store, are generally satisfied, and are likely to continue to shop at the retailer in the future. Over time, a retailer wants to maximize the number of these customers who become angels and minimize the number who turn into demons.

Figure 9.2. Normal Distribution of Customer Satisfaction

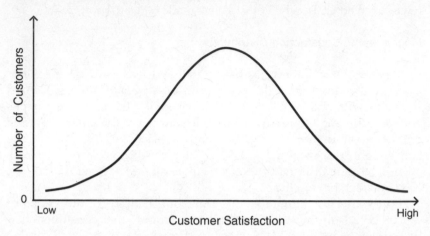

Thinking in terms of the aggregate level of satisfaction – and, ultimately, the value – of the firm's customer base can provide retail managers with an important perspective on building relationships and growing the business. A company like Starbucks serves a lot of customers, some of whom will be dissatisfied with the service they receive and some of whom will be delighted. The impact of a Dorosin on the company's performance is negligible when his views represent only a tiny fraction of the overall customer base. More generally, when retailers satisfy most of their customers and build strong long-term relationships, they pave the way for future success and insulate against the inevitability of service failures, negative critical incidents, demons, and detractors.

Chapter Ten

Customer Loyalty

Every day, more than 1.5 million customers shop at Best Buy. In 2004, CEO Brad Anderson estimated that demon customers accounted for about 20 percent of these shopping trips – in other words, every year the company had more than one hundred million customer visits it considered undesirable.[1] These customers did not engage in illegal activities; however, they abused the customer service policies and cost the company significant amounts of money. For example, some demon customers would buy products with mail-in rebates, collect the rebate, and then return the product. They would later buy the same product back after Best Buy had restocked it at a discounted returned-product price. The company found that some demons used Best Buy's low-price pledge to demand that the retailer match extremely low prices they had found on obscure websites. Other demon customers aggressively purchased products that Best Buy was selling at very low prices – for example, to match a competitor's sale price or to generate store traffic – and then resold those products on eBay.

Best Buy also knew that another 20 percent of its customers were angels.[2] In fact, these were the customers the company hoped to entice into the store with low prices and wow with a service experience that included lenient return and price-matching policies. What Best Buy found, however, was that angels did not enjoy its policies as much as demons abused them. In response, the company began to tighten up its procedures and build systems that were designed to deter demons. For example, it instituted a restocking fee for product returns, clarified its price-matching guarantee, and relied less on price promotions to generate traffic. In addition, the company developed a segmentation scheme that focused on shoppers that it believed would be attracted by

the revised value proposition and be unlikely to generate demon customers. Most importantly, Best Buy began to focus on building relationships with angel customers in ways that would not appeal to demons
– that is, it put more emphasis on the ESE components of the retail
value proposition and less on building traffic through price discounts.
For example, during the critical holiday shopping season, Best Buy introduced a two-hour private shopping event for its most valuable shoppers. The top two hundred shoppers in each store received a personal
phone call from the store's general manager inviting them to attend
the event. Rather than fight crowds and stand in long lines to purchase
Christmas presents, invitees had one-on-one service from employees,
live product demonstrations from manufacturers, and the opportunity
to win vendor-sponsored door prizes. This type of event was specifically designed to enhance the experience for angel customers, while
providing very little for demon customers only interested in paying the
lowest possible price.

Demons in the Data

Of course, Best Buy has been pushed into exploring a system that provides detailed customer valuations because it operates in a rapidly
changing marketplace with powerful and agile competitors that have
been built on world-class information technology (think, for example,
of Apple and Amazon). This approach does not guarantee success, but
it does point toward the future of retail competition. If other retailers
want to build on Best Buy's preliminary efforts to appeal to angels
and deter demons, they will need to develop their own systems for
data management and analysis. In fact, from designing the store environment to product selection management to customer engagement,
a successful retail value proposition depends on the retailer's ability
to collect information about the consumers it serves. Back when most
people shopped at a neighborhood general store, merchants knew their
customers personally and were able to cater to their individual tastes.
However, as retailers aggressively expanded both the number and the
size of their stores, the scope of their businesses quickly outgrew their
ability to know customers as individuals.

To compensate for the lack of personal relationships, retailers have
become experts at using aggregate level data such as surveys and point-
of-sale systems to understand segments of consumers. Scanner panel
data are particularly useful in capturing behavioral information that

provides insight into several key areas of retail management, including location decisions, product design, product assortment, category management, sales, promotions, pricing, and advertising campaigns. At the same time, increasingly sophisticated survey techniques allow retailers to gather more accurate psychographic information, such as customer satisfaction data, as well as more general consumer attitudes, intentions, and preferences. National level census survey data collected by the United States Census Bureau have given retailers extremely valuable geographic and demographic information on current and potential customers. That wealth of aggregate-level data does not, however, truly replace the deep understanding that comes from knowing individual customers on a personal level. If retailers want to get to know individuals, they need to have some way to identify and value specific shoppers within their databases. For many retailers, the solution to the problem of collecting data at the level of the individual consumer is a loyalty program.

Loyalty Programs

Originally, many loyalty card programs were simply a way to offer repeat customers a volume discount – for example, buy ten ice cream cones at Stone Cold Creamery and receive the next one for free. The major drawback of this type of loyalty program is its anonymity – that is, the company does not learn anything about the customer.

Retailers quickly realized they could offer consumers programs that went beyond volume discounts and allowed them to collect critical data on the customers they served. Following the example set by the airline industry, many retailers created programs that allow consumers to collect points they can later redeem for rewards such as travel and merchandise. Companies give program members a card with a unique identifier to track the details of all related spending. For example, companies can record RFM and CLV data and link that information to the geographic, demographic, and product preference details that consumers provide when they join the program. Over time, the retailer can build profiles for increasingly well-defined segments – or, in some cases, even individual customers – that allow it to personalize the product offer. Harrah's casinos, for example, use this type of data to decide what price to charge a customer who calls to make a hotel reservation. While angel customers may be given a complimentary room, other guests are charged a rate that varies with the expected value of their stay. Demon customers may even be denied access to a room. Similarly, Best Buy uses the data from its Reward Zone loyalty program to identify the customers it invites to its private shopping events.

In fact, research indicates that loyalty points programs create a competitive advantage in several different critical retail competencies. In a classic study of Tesco's Clubcard, JP Morgan Cazenove concluded that the U.K. grocer benefits from its industry-leading loyalty program in a variety of ways.[3] For example, having data on individual customers' transactions allowed the company to more accurately identify trends in consumer behavior. Such insights allowed for superior location decisions, as well as more precisely designed and executed marketing communications and promotional campaigns. As a result, the company dramatically reduced its reliance on mass media advertising and instead focused on personalized direct marketing that effectively generated traffic from target customer segments. In addition, using Clubcard data, Tesco excelled at cross-category selling, as well as inventory and shelf-space management, because it was better able to predict what consumers wanted to buy at a particular location. Most importantly, Tesco leveraged its superior understanding of its customers to succeed without resorting to large-scale price discounting in the United Kingdom's highly competitive grocery and general merchandise market.

Types of Loyalty Programs

Since retail loyalty programs were first introduced, companies have tried out a variety of approaches and program designs in an attempt to better reward loyal customers and collect critical data. Loyalty programs continue to evolve in response to competition, consumer preferences, and corporate objectives. At a general level, however, retail loyalty-card programs can be classified as one of three generic types, based on the degree of collaboration between sponsoring organizations. Programs such as Best Buy's Reward Zone, Amazon Prime, and Shoppers Optimum are proprietary – that is, a single retailer administers the program and manages the data. Others use a partnership model in which two organizations join forces to promote the card and share the data. The "Crossover Rewards" partnership between Starwood and Delta is one example of this type of program. Finally, retailers can join forces across industries and retailer sectors to create coalition programs such as AAdvantage and Plenti (by American Express). Each approach has advantages and disadvantages that should be considered as part of the customer engagement component of a retailer's value proposition.

THE PROPRIETARY PROGRAM

Sephora's Beauty Insider rewards program is one of the most successful proprietary retail initiatives. When customers spend a dollar, they
receive one point. When they accumulate 100 points, they can redeem
them for a deluxe sample with their next purchase. At 500 points,
Sephora's customers receive a curated set of products. Members who
spend $350 annually earn VIB (Very Important Beauty) status and those
who spend $1,000 in a year are part of the VIB Rouge club. VIB mem-
bers get first dibs on new products and advance access to sales and VIB-
only shopping events. Rouge members also get free shipping, exclusive
access to Rouge events, and gifts.

Best Buy (Reward Zone), Walgreens (Balance Rewards), Tesco (Clubcard), and many other retailers have also developed their own proprietary programs. Going it alone has several important advantages. First,
proprietary programs tend to be relatively simple and straightforward
– earn points for dollars spent and redeem those points for discounts
on store merchandise. The points reward customers for their loyalty and
give them an incentive to continue to shop at the store. Second, there
is no brand confusion; the relationship is between the customer and a
single retailer. Any loyalty the program creates is directly connected to
that retailer and is not shared with other program sponsors. Third, and
most importantly, the company has complete control over the program
and the customer data. The company knows who the program members
are, what they buy, how many points they collect, when they redeem the
points (and for what), and how the program affects sales and profitability
on a customer-by-customer basis. For many organizations, this unam-
biguous control is the primary reason to go with a proprietary model.

However, administration costs offset the advantages of clarity and
control in a proprietary program. When a retailer decides to create and
manage its own loyalty card, it is solely responsible for marketing and
managing that program. For many retailers, such programs are simply
too expensive. Although retail chains with national scale in businesses
with a large volume of regular repeat purchases – such as Sephora,
Walgreens, Tesco, and Best Buy – may be able to achieve a solid return
on investment in a proprietary program, many other organizations are
better off in partnerships or coalitions.

THE PARTNERSHIP PROGRAM

Partnership programs tend to be between two organizations that are
interested in the same customer segments and able to bring different

types of value to the customer relationship. Most commonly, loyalty partnerships are between banks and other consumer marketers. For example, Starwood partnered with Delta to create the Crossover Rewards. Through this arrangement, both companies are able to give customers loyal to Starwood and Delta benefits that extend beyond what either program can do individually. As their website says "Earn Starpoints® and get extra benefits when you fly with Delta; earn miles and enjoy added hotel benefits when you stay with SPG." The partnership model makes it easier for the loyalty program to gain critical mass, as it is promoted by two consumer marketing organizations that are otherwise unrelated to each other. When successful, both organizations have a chance to build relationships with a new set of customers. From the customers' perspective, the partnership means additional opportunities to earn points and redeem rewards.

The disadvantages of partnership programs arise from potential imbalances in the return on investment that the partners are able to achieve. This can happen on the cost side, if the program is more expensive for one of the partners to administer, as well as on the revenue side, if the benefits are not equally distributed and balanced with the costs. There is also the risk of brand confusion if the program becomes overly complex, with points that can be collected and redeemed in too many different ways.

THE COALITION PROGRAM

In the United States, programs like AAdvantage and Plenti (by American Express) offer a broad coalition approach to loyalty. These programs allow customers to carry a single card and keep track of points and rewards through a single program, rather than belonging to many proprietary or partnership programs. From the consumer's perspective, this is an important simplification that can significantly improve the shopping experience. Retailers involved in such programs benefit from substantially lower administration costs. More importantly, joining a large coalition program instantly expands the retailer's reach into U.S. households. An especially powerful advantage of the coalition approach is the company's ability to get to know not only its customers but also consumers who are not yet customers. These data can be critically important for retailers that want to expand their market share and acquire new customers.

One of the major disadvantages of the coalition model is that not all brands benefit equally from being sponsors of the program. The

AAdvantage program, for example, has come a long way from the days when it was all about American Airlines' efforts in marketing and customer retention. Today, the program boasts a large number of associated organizations from the retail, travel, and financial service industries. However, the brand remains closely tied to American Airlines, and for many consumers the primary benefit of being a member is achieving top-tier traveler status with the airline. It can be very challenging for a coalition program to balance value with cost across dozens of partners of different sizes in diverse industries and competitive positions.

A related problem is getting the sponsors within the program to work cooperatively, even though they all have their own unique value propositions and corporate objectives. In addition, some retailers have expressed concern about the nature of the loyalty that a coalition program cultivates. Are consumers loyal to the individual sponsors' brands – for example, to Macy's, Rite Aid, and Exxon – or are they loyal to the Plenti program itself? Retailers in a coalition risk contributing to program loyalty rather than building their own customer equity. Finally, the use and management of customer data can also become a contentious issue in a coalition program. It is important to be very clear about who owns the data and how they can be shared within the coalition, respecting both confidential corporate information and the privacy of consumers.

When Customers Pay Money to Be Loyal

Amazon is a unique retailer in many respects. It doesn't have physical stores; it sells products in a mind-boggling variety of categories and breadth of SKUs; and it runs a loyalty program that loses billions of dollars per year even though it costs $99 to join. The program offers consumers free two-day shipping, unlimited movie and TV watching with Prime Instant Video, more than a million songs, free photo storage, and special sales events. Unlike traditional points-based loyalty programs, Prime doesn't require members to save and then redeem points for rewards. Instead, it charges a fee in exchange for specific services. Of course, Prime members have a strong incentive to shop at Amazon and are regularly engaging with the company (they shop with Amazon about 50 percent more frequently than other customers). This helps explain why Amazon's 40 million Prime members spend on average about $1,500 per year, as compared to regular customers who spend $625 annually.[4]

The membership fee approach is similar to Costco's model (although you don't have to be a Prime member to shop at Amazon) or the rewards program of retailers like Barnes and Noble. In essence, asking customers to pay money up front creates an incentive for them to be loyal to "earn" back their investment and maybe even gain more in rewards than they pay in fees. Asking customers to pay money to make them more loyal may sound counter-intuitive, but as Costco and Amazon have demonstrated, many consumers are eager to join. In Costco's case the company makes almost all of its profits from its membership fees,[5] and 45 percent of Amazon's U.S. customers have opted in to the Prime program.

Assets versus Liabilities

Loyal customers appreciate being recognized for their value to the company and rewarded for their repeat business. Most consumers who join a retail loyalty program do so because of the short-term benefits they expect to receive. Programs that seem to provide little value or require too much effort are unlikely to achieve critical mass and retain consumers over the long term. The ultimate goal of a loyalty program is to increase the value of the company's customers by improving profit margins and retention rates while decreasing the costs of acquiring new shoppers. Programs that are successful in this endeavor enhance a retailer's most valuable asset: its customer base. In other words, with an up-front investment in the loyalty program, the retailer creates an asset that provides an ongoing stream of future cash flow.

Unfortunately, too many loyalty programs have instead turned the company's customers into liabilities. When consumers collect points, the retailer is making a promise of a future reward. In fact, the idea behind a loyalty program is to influence the consumer's decision process by offering points alongside their purchases. The consumer intends to redeem those points for a discount or other merchandise – that is, the consumer makes a purchase today and expects the company to pay them back for their loyalty later. For example, in 2003, United Airlines estimated that its loyalty program represented a liability of more than $700 million in unredeemed points for free flights.[6] In the United States, the annual value of the rewards points issued to consumers is estimated at almost $50 billion.[7] Over time many programs have had to adjust their rules around earning and redeeming points to manage, at least in part, the outstanding liabilities their points programs have created. From the consumer's perspective, believing that a retailer's loyalty program promises one thing and finding out that it delivers another results in an overall experience that fails to meet expectations. In an effort to contain the liability, these loyalty programs end up creating dissatisfied customers.

Steven Shugan makes this point and asks: Are these loyalty programs shams? In an article in *Marketing Science*, he examines the premise that loyalty programs can create true customer loyalty. In fact, research suggests that this premise is incorrect.[8] True customer loyalty is built over time as the retail value proposition continues to meet or exceed consumers' expectations and strong relationships develop. All a loyalty program can do is provide an incentive for the customer to continue to shop at the retailer, and as the relationship develops, the retailer can use the data it collects through the program to improve and personalize its value proposition. If a rewards program is to build real loyalty, it will do so through the enhanced customer knowledge that the retailer is able to extract from the data it collects. Retailers focused on gimmicks and short-term promotions risk losing sight of the real drivers of value – environment, selection, and true customer engagement. A good retail loyalty program is not an attempt to compensate for a weak value proposition. Instead, it is an opportunity to enhance the organization's understanding of the customers responsible for its success. The best loyalty programs aim to increase each of these aspects of retail revenue generation over the lifetime of the customer. They can do so through recognizing and rewarding customers; but more importantly, the data they collect can be used to increase the relevance of the retailers to individuals, or at least to small segments of customers.

Trial and Error

Like most aspects of retail management, loyalty programs are not one-time initiatives. To be successful over the long term it is important to continue to evolve the program to meet changing market conditions and consumer demand. For example, although historically many retail programs have focused on the points-style loyalty card, advances in technology have introduced new approaches that use mobile phones and even biometric scanners (e.g., a finger scan during the checkout process). The basic structure of a loyalty program can change over time, and an initially proprietary program may eventually expand to include a partner or coalition. A points-program database originally designed to identify angels may be used to filter out demons.

It is also important for retailers to keep a careful eye on the use of loyalty program points and discounts over time. Even the most successful and sophisticated loyalty programs have been known to make promotional mistakes. In *Scoring Points*, Humby, Hunt, and Phillips recount the now infamous story of the "Banana Man of Worcester." In the late 1990s, a physicist named Phil Calcott bought more than three thousand bananas, weighing over 900 pounds, from Tesco in two days. He then gave the bananas away for free on the street, which earned him the nickname Banana Man. As it turned out, Calcott's motivation was not purely philanthropic. He realized that Tesco's promotion for three pounds of bananas at £1.17 awarded £1.25 worth of Clubcard points. He engaged in "fruit arbitrage" to make a little money while he gave the bananas away for free. In the end, any loss Tesco took on the promotion was more than offset by the positive publicity Calcott generated. Nevertheless, promotional errors open the door to demon customers who want to get something for nothing and do little to create loyalty among the angel customers retailers want to attract.

Relevance

As important as recognition and rewards are to customers in the short term, the real value of a loyalty program is in its potential to dramatically enhance the relevance of the interactions between retailers and consumers. Historically, consumer marketing relied heavily on mass advertising through radio, television, and newspapers. By definition, these media channels reach a broad audience and can only target the largest and most general consumer segments. As a result, most of the marketing messages that a consumer receives every day are irrelevant. The in-store shopping experience is equally generic; because a successful store serves thousands of consumers, it has to be designed to accommodate them all. Similarly, most products are designed to be "big hits" – that is, appeal to a large segment of consumers – which means that they are not tailored to specific individual preferences. In combination, mass advertising, generic store designs, and "big hit" products result in value propositions that are only marginally relevant to many consumers. Recent advances in manufacturing technology, omnichannel retailing, and customer data management have opened the door to a new era of relevant retailing built on the principles of personalization and mass customization.

Personalization

When Piggly Wiggly introduced the first self-service grocery store, it dramatically changed the retail experience. Much to the surprise of many retailers at the time, customers were happy to give up the extra attention and service they had traditionally received and select their own items off the shelf in exchange for lower prices and an expanded selection of products. Interestingly, Clarence Saunders, Piggly Wiggly's founder and the man responsible for ushering in this new era of retail, spent the rest of his career trying to create yet another business model that captured the best of both worlds – an automated store that improved the efficiency of the shopping process without the added cost of additional employees. Unfortunately, in the late 1930s, technology was not sufficiently advanced to make this dream a reality. Today, however, the technology does exist – in both physical and online stores – to create an efficient, automated, and personalized shopping experience.

Imagine, for example, that a consumer walks into her neighborhood Road Runner Sports and finds the entire store laid out according to her preferences. She is a size six, and so only shoes from sizes five to seven are on display. She is a cross-country runner, and so the shelves are populated with sneakers designed for running long distances outdoors. She prefers some brands to others, and so the shoes are ordered from her most to least favorite. Although this environment has been designed to focus on shoes appropriate for cross-country running, the store has also stocked several related items ranging from clothing to pedometers that may also be of interest to her. Finally, an expert in running shoe fit and comfort is available to answer questions and make recommendations. The next customer who visits the store wants a new watch that will report his heart rate and track his training progress. When he enters the store, the layout is built around a technology display that prominently features relevant watches. In fact, every time a customer enters the store, the layout changes and the shopping environment changes to match his or her needs, desires, and preferences.

For a bricks-and-mortar store, a customer-by-customer redesign is fantasy; however, by incorporating online shopping and augmented reality, retailers today can create environments that are uniquely tailored to specific consumers. Amazon and Netflix have played a leading role in building online shopping environments driven by their knowledge about individual customers. Based on prior behavior, customers' self-reported preferences, and the preferences of similar consumers, these websites present each individual with an interface designed specifically for them.

In the bricks-and-mortar world, Barnes and Noble uses the data it has collected on the value of individual customers and the types of books they prefer to read and is able to develop personalized direct mail campaigns and newsletters. It can create hundreds of unique customer segments and can send each of those segments a different version of a direct mail or e-mail newsletter. As an example, for Harry Potter fans, the books and related merchandise are prominently promoted. For customers who have not been in the store recently but have previously purchased books on personal finance, the newsletter can provide coupons for the latest publications related to retirement planning. Another version of the promotional material might focus on people who have a track record of buying travel books. These segments could be further divided up to ensure that the more price-sensitive customers received coupons along with their newsletter, while less price-sensitive customers did not.

Tesco has developed an approach that aims to fill what it sees as the "hole in the basket."[9] In its quarterly mail-out, in addition to sending out coupons for items the customer has purchased in the past, Tesco includes coupons for products the customer should be buying but is not. This prediction is based on Clubcard data about what similar consumers purchase. This approach is conceptually similar to what Amazon and Netflix do when they recommend books or movies to one customer based on what similar consumers read and watch. That type of personalized offer increases the probability of purchase and contributes to the retailer's ability to exceed customers' expectations. When successful, personalization can identify and promote products consumers want, even before they know they want them.

Mass Customization

In addition to creating more satisfied consumers, collecting data on individual consumers can make retailers' inventory management processes more efficient, enabling them to predict more accurately what customers will buy. In fact, as manufacturing technology improves and retailers continue to develop new ways to deliver products to consumers, they can push inventories to minimal levels and focus on custom-built products from a store of raw materials. This is the idea behind mass customization. In essence, it aims to facilitate the efficient production of items that are cost-effectively customized to the preferences of individual consumers.

When Henry Ford created the assembly line and dramatically improved the efficiency with which his company could manufacture cars, he proudly announced that customers could have his automobiles in any color they wanted as long as that color was black. In other words, in exchange for allowing customers to purchase a quality product at a low price, the assembly line model traded off the ability to build a large variety of cars for the ability to build standardized cars more efficiently. In the century since Ford revolutionized manufacturing, the mass production process has become increasingly flexible and efficient. Today, automobile manufacturers from Ford to BMW offer consumers the option of buying a car that has been customized to their individual preferences using a variety of flexible components. On a smaller scale, retailers such as Build-A-Bear charge customers a premium price for the opportunity to custom build their own products from a selection of parts. Starbucks sells thousands of unique drinks that can be mass customized to the tastes of individual consumers through different combinations of milk, espresso, and a few other ingredients.

Privacy

The value of personalized and mass-customized relevant offers based on data about individuals can be extraordinary. Customers receive products and services that closely match their needs, and retailers build stronger relationships. However, with an ever-greater amount of personal consumer data comes an ever-greater responsibility to safeguard that information. In addition, consumers are increasingly aware that they are making a trade-off between the value they receive and the data they surrender. Retailers that misuse or misappropriate consumer data risk violating customers' trust and wiping out any investments that have been made in relationship building. As a result, protecting consumer information and using it appropriately are of paramount importance to the future of individual-level consumer marketing.

Companies such as Google have promoted a corporate philosophy of "don't be evil" that has informed their increasingly transparent approach to the management of personal data. Apple has taken a different approach and is advocating against collecting and storing this type of customer data. Retailers such as Tesco have built their loyalty programs on a written promise to guard personal information that concludes with the statement: "If at any time you would like your details taken off the database, we will do so immediately."[10] This approach pressures Tesco to ensure that consumers believe it is worth giving up their personal information in exchange for the value the retailer provides through personalized offers and an improved retail value proposition. To be competitive, retailers need to be increasingly sophisticated in their use of quantitative data. That data, however, should support and complement, rather than replace, managerial judgment.

PART 5

Putting It All Together

Chapter Eleven

Retail Pricing

Alexander Turney Stewart made his name as a retail innovator. In 1846, he opened the Marble Dry Goods Palace, the first modern-style department store, on the northeast corner of Chambers and Broadway in New York City.[1] The exterior of the building was five stories of cream-colored marble topped by an eighty-foot dome. To attract customers into the store, Stewart pioneered the use of street-level plate-glass windows to display merchandise. Inside, both luxury and everyday goods were sold under the domed roof in a large rotunda. The Marble Palace is credited with introducing the first in-store fashion shows, which took place in that space. Stewart was also widely revered for being one of the first mass-merchandise discounters to use sales and promotions to attract female shoppers and keep inventory flowing, even during difficult economic times.[2] When he died in 1876, he was the second richest man in America, after oil tycoon John D. Rockefeller. Today, the Marble Palace building still stands at 280 Broadway and is occupied by New York City municipal offices.

Yet, for all of Stewart's accomplishments, his most important innovation was fixed product prices. He was the first to eliminate haggling and mark each product with a set price.[3] At the time, other retailers negotiated with each customer to establish a price for most product sales. Stewart recognized that consumers were unhappy with this adversarial shopping experience, which many found frustrating and inefficient. Other retailers soon followed Stewart's lead, and within a few decades fixed pricing became a standard retail practice.

The historical approach to haggling over every sale recognized that every customer has a different willingness to pay for the same products. By negotiating the price on each sale, the retailer maximized its profitability on a transaction-by-transaction basis. The problem with this approach, however, was that it focused on the value of the sale rather than on the value of each customer. Stewart recognized that customers satisfied with their shopping experience were worth much more than a single sale and tried to build his business around that philosophy. He designed his Marble Palace to be an inviting shopping environment with a broad selection of products and a strong focus on engaging customers with innovative displays and fashion shows – that is, a compelling retail value proposition. Importantly, Stewart recognized that once the ESE components of that value proposition were in place, pricing played a balancing role. In other words, the fixed price Stewart set on each item he offered for sale was what he asked in exchange for the value the Marble Palace provided.

Today, retailers continue to struggle with effective pricing tactics and strategies. In fact, given the focus many merchants put on pricing decisions, it might seem strange to address pricing only at the end of a book on crafting a retail value proposition. Pricing remains critically important because it is the financial context in which customers decide if the value offered is worth the cost of purchase. If consumers believe the price of the product is worth paying in exchange for the value they receive, then the transaction is likely to proceed. If the retailer's value proposition is not sufficient to justify the price, then the probability of purchase declines significantly. Compelling prices are those that the consumer believes are lower than the perceived value of the goods purchased.

That means, however, that the right price is a function of the customers' view of the value proposition and cannot be effectively finalized until the mix of ESE components has been crafted. Great retailers are able to design the shopping environment, manage product selection, and engage customers at a cost much lower than the value that consumers see in the overall offer and, as a result, well below the price that they are willing to pay.

Getting the Price Right

Retailers should not compete on price alone. Lowering prices to gain revenue puts unwanted pressure on profitability. The only player who can win in that game is the one with the lowest costs. Today most retailers work hard to be more efficient and keep costs to a minimum. As a result, no one retailer can be the cost leader across all of its products all the time. Even attempting to do so means minimizing profit margins and in the long term substantially reduces the overall value of any retail enterprise. For example, although Walmart is the world's largest company and has more than two and a half times Apple's revenue, it has only about one-third of Apple's stock market value.

That is not to say that different retail organizations do not put a different emphasis on the extent to which they want to occupy that price leadership position. Clearly, Walmart's focus on keeping costs down and prices low is a big part of its position as the world's largest corporation. Yet, even with its advantages in size, real estate, technology, and supply chain management, Walmart does not want to offer only the lowest price. This is reflected in the recent change in the company's slogan from "Always low prices" to "Save Money. Live Better."[4] For customers, the buying process is not about price, it is about value. Put another way, consumers care about low prices to the extent that those prices let them "Live Better." Great retail pricing, then, matches the asking price to the value offered.

Supply and Demand

Introductory economics textbooks define price as the *money price* – that is, the number of dollars that must be given up in exchange for a product. Many factors come into play when a consumer decides whether or not to buy a particular product at a given money price. These include the current price of the good, the price of related and substitute goods, the expected future prices for the good, his personal budget and income, and his preferences. Microeconomics also indicates that the price regulates both the demand and supply of goods. As prices rise, demand tends to fall, and it becomes increasingly likely that products will be left unsold on the shelf. As prices fall, demand tends to rise, and it becomes increasingly likely that stores will sell out of that good and customers will be unable to buy the products they desire. The goal for a retailer is to set an *equilibrium price* at which demand equals supply. By doing so, consumers pay the highest price they are willing to pay for the last item sold and the retailer receives the lowest price at which they are willing to sell the product.

In practice, however, it can be challenging for retailers to apply these concepts. First, it is notoriously difficult to make accurate projections of consumer demand in competitive and evolving retail product categories. Second, even when demand might be predicted fairly accurately – for example, in staple items like eggs and milk or black running shorts – retailers cannot easily determine supply at the industry level because the competition continually evolves. New competitors might enter the market and increase the local supply. The competition might also use staple items as *loss leaders* – that is, it might sell products below cost to generate traffic. In fact, both supply and demand can change in ways that are unpredictable and difficult to recognize in time to inform pricing decisions. Changes in consumers' preferences and the local or global economy can affect demand. Crop failures, raw material shortages, and natural disasters can disrupt supply. As a result, although the microeconomic principles of supply and demand may help to structure thinking about industry trends, they tend to have little value in day-to-day pricing decisions.

Cost-Based Pricing

In practice, many retailers price their products based on the cost of the item. As long as the retailer is able to accurately account for the relevant costs, setting a price is as simple as deciding how much to *mark up* the product. The markup is the difference between the cost of the product and the retail price. For example, if a T-shirt costs $30 and sells for $60, it has a $30 markup. Some retailers calculate the markup percentage based on the product's *cost* using the following formula.

Markup Percentage on Cost =
  (Retail Price – Cost of Merchandise)/Cost of Merchandise
T-shirt Example:
  Markup Percentage Based on Cost = ($60 – $30)/$30

In the T-shirt example, this formula indicates that the markup percentage on cost is 100 percent. However, to be consistent with gross margin percentage calculations, most retailers prefer to calculate the markup based on the *retail selling price*, as follows:

Markup Percentage on Retail Price =
  (Retail Price – Cost of Merchandise)/Retail Price
T-shirt Example: Markup Percentage Based on Retail Price =
  ($60 – $30)/$60

Therefore, the markup percentage on the retail price of a T-shirt is 50 percent. The difference in the markup percentage based on cost versus retail price is in the denominator. In both cases, the dollar markup is $30.

Now, assume this retailer would like to maintain a 50 percent mark-up on the retail price across every T-shirt it sells. To calculate the price of other T-shirts, it would use the following formula:

Retail Price = Cost of Product/(1 – Markup Percentage on Retail Price)
$23 T-shirt Example: Retail Price = $23/(1 – 0.5)

As a result, when the cost of a different T-shirt is $23, then the retail price is $46. If the retailer decides it wants to apply a higher markup percentage on the retail price for the T-shirt that costs $23 – for example, 65 percent rather than 50 percent – the retail price increases to $65.71. In practice, the markup percentage a retailer aims to achieve changes by product, category, and other factors, such as variations across individual store locations. Most buyers and category managers, however, aim to achieve an average markup percentage across their entire inventory. That average must account for both the initial markup and any discounts or markdowns that occur when a product is put on sale. Today, many retailers use sophisticated merchandising optimization software to assist managers in deciding when – and to what extent – to mark down products.

The major advantage of cost-based pricing is that once the retailer calculates the cost of the product, setting a price is relatively straightforward. In addition, the retailer controls its profitability by ensuring that the price of each product includes the desired markup. A simple cost-based approach to pricing, however, does not take the retail value proposition into account. Instead, it sets the price based on the product's cost and hopes the customer sees value in the item (see figure 11.1). As a result, the merchant runs the risk of pricing products at a level above the perceived value, in which case sales will suffer, or choosing a price point below the perceived value, in which case profits will suffer. For example, if customers are willing to pay $80 for a T-shirt that cost the retailer $23, then the company would be leaving money on the table if it sold the shirt for $65. Along the same lines, if customers only see $45 of value in that T-shirt, pricing it at $65 means it will not sell.

Value-Based Pricing

When a retailer determines product prices based on the value the consumer perceives in the offer, it follows a value-based approach to pricing. In contrast to cost-based pricing, this approach begins with the customer. Later in this chapter, I examine *dynamic pricing*, which

Figure 11.1. The Chain of Logic in Cost-Based Pricing

Cost ⟶ Price ⟶ Value ⟶ Consumer

attempts to set a value-based price for each individual customer; but first I look at value-based pricing applied to store-level decisions.

To set a value-based price, the retailer needs to estimate the value its consumer base sees in its products. Data of this type are normally acquired through market research, such as in-store experiments, surveys, or focus groups. Using that information, the retailer sets the price for the product. If the price of the product is not sufficiently higher than the cost – that is, if the retail price does not include an acceptable markup – then the company is unlikely to offer the product for sale. If selling the product is important to the retailer's competitive position or target segments, it will either find ways to reduce the cost of the product or sell the product as a loss leader (in hopes that the customers who buy it will buy other products at an acceptable markup). The philosophy behind value-based pricing reverses the chain of logic as compared to a cost-based approach (see figure 11.2).

The advantage of this approach is that the retailer accounts for the overall value proposition as the consumer sees it, rather than focusing solely on the cost of producing and selling the product. When properly executed, value-based pricing can be critical to the success of a retail venture. Imagine, for example, that when Starbucks first began to sell its espresso drinks, it decided to price its coffee using a cost-based approach. The coffee itself is relatively inexpensive and is only a small part of the Starbucks value proposition. A cost-based price would have failed to capture the premium value that consumers see in the overall experience of the café environment, customized product selection, and personalized customer engagement, which differentiated Starbucks from other coffee merchants and led to its success. Other retail brands that have crafted a unique value proposition – from Kroger to LUSH Cosmetics to lululemon – would also be leaving money on the table if they took a purely cost-based approach.

The downside of the value-based approach is the slippery nature of consumers' perceptions of value and the difficulty in accurately estimating value that customers see in a product. In 1981, Nobel Laureate Daniel Kahneman and his mentor Amos Tversky investigated the

Figure 11.2. The Chain of Logic in Value-Based Pricing

Consumer ⟶ Value ⟶ Price ⟶ Cost

propensity of consumers to make an effort to save $5 based on the original price of the product.[5] To do so, they presented a group of respondents with a consumption scenario. One half of the group was given the price in ( ) and the other half of the group was given the price in [ ], as follows:

> Imagine that you are about to purchase a jacket for ($125) [$15] and a calculator for ($15) [$125]. The calculator salesman informs you that the calculator you wish to buy is on sale for ($10) [$120] at the other branch of the store, located 20 minutes' drive away. Would you make the trip to the other store?

Regardless of the price of the jacket and whether the other store was selling a $15 calculator for $10 or a $125 calculator for $120, the consumer could save $5 by traveling twenty minutes to the other store. Kahneman and Tversky found that 68 percent of respondents in the $15 calculator group were willing to make the trip to save $5, but only 29 percent of respondents in the $125 calculator group were willing to do the same. Many other researchers have since replicated this result and extended it to other consumption contexts. In one notable example, economist Richard Thaler asked a group of participants in an executive development program who identified themselves as regular beer drinkers to respond to the following scenario.[6] Again, participants were randomly assigned to one of two groups, and each group received a slightly different version of the scenario, represented by ( ) and [ ] below:

> You are lying on the beach on a hot day. All you have to drink is ice water. For the last hour you have been thinking about how much you would enjoy a nice cold bottle of your favorite brand of beer. A companion gets up to go make a phone call and offers to bring back a beer from the only nearby place where beer is sold (a fancy resort hotel) [a small, run-down grocery store]. He says that the beer might be expensive and so asks how much you are willing to pay for the beer. He says that he will buy the beer if it costs as much as or less than the price you state. But if it costs more

than the price you state he will not buy it. You trust your friend, and there is no possibility of bargaining with (the bartender) [store owner]. What price do you tell him?[7]

Although all that differed between the scenarios was the place where the beer would be purchased, consumers' average willingness to pay differed dramatically between the two groups. Those given the fancy resort hotel version were willing to pay $2.65, or 77 percent more than the run-down grocery store respondents, who were willing to pay only $1.50.

The evidence is clear: the value consumers place on money and products changes according to context. This can make value-based pricing a challenge for retailers with many stores that sell products across many categories to many different consumer segments. In addition to differences in perceived value across contexts, retailers may also face differences in perceived value across people. In other words, some beer drinkers are willing to pay more than $2.65 for a beer from a fancy hotel, and some are not. Retailers that take a value-based approach must use pricing tactics that address these variations.

For example, if the differences in willingness-to-pay can be captured through geographic segmentation, then the retailer can price based on the unique customer segments served by different store locations. If perceived value varies between segments based on factors other than geography, the retailer needs a different set of tactics for price discrimination across consumers within one location. For fashion merchandise, one way to resolve this problem is to open the season with high prices and mark down the merchandise over time. In this way, consumers who put a premium value on the newest fashions pay higher prices to purchase those items sooner, while customers who wait until the end of the season can get the same goods at a lower price. Retailers may also use coupons to provide a lower price to customers willing to find and redeem them. Consumers who do not make that effort, or to whom the coupons are not offered, pay the higher price.

High-Low Promotional Pricing

When a retailer uses sales to discount prices, generate store traffic, and move inventory, it follows a high-low pricing strategy. This approach aims to capitalize on the fact that different consumer segments are willing to pay different amounts for the same merchandise. During periods of higher prices, the store tries to capture more profitable sales from less price-sensitive customers. When the retailer puts those same products on sale, it aims to increase its sales volume by appealing to more price-sensitive shoppers. Historically, retailers have used high-low pricing to clear inventory at the end of a season or share discounts from manufacturers and suppliers. Today, increased competition and a larger segment of price-sensitive consumers pressure many retailers into using sales and price discounts to build or maintain their market position.

In fact, one of the key benefits of enhanced cooperation within the supply chain is that retailers and manufacturers more effectively collaborate on sales promotions and price discounts as part of improved category management and shopper marketing processes. Over the years, retailers have been very creative in the design and execution of price-based promotions. Nevertheless, most promotions can be classified into one of two general categories: (1) products sold at a reduced price – for example, 10 percent off the regular price, including time-restricted or introductory offers; and (2) products sold at the regular price, but with "extra added" – for example, buy one, get one free (BOGO). Other types of promotions use price as an incentive for customers to try a different brand of product. Private label products use discounts to attract consumers who normally buy national brands. Market-leading national brands use discounts to attract customers who normally buy less expensive alternatives, including private labels.

Each year, retailers spend billions on price-based promotions, yet it is not clear that they are successful. For example, in 2004, Shuba Srinivasan found that price-based promotions do not typically have long-term value for either retailers or manufacturers, even after he accounted for cross-category shopping and the impact on store traffic.[8] Although promotions can increase revenues, they hurt overall profitability. Given this impact, it is not surprising that related research, led by Koen Pauwels, found that price promotions tend to diminish the long-term shareholder value of retail corporations.[9]

A big part of the problem with promotions is that they teach consumers that the product has less value than they thought. For example, consider a consumer who happily buys jeans from Banana Republic for $110. The customer gives his e-mail address to the retailer during the checkout process, and he begins to receive electronic coupons and promotional offers through which the same jeans cost less than $70. In fact, every couple of weeks, he receives another offer from Banana Republic for a discount on merchandise. Although he initially saw $110 worth of value in his jeans, over time, the company convinces him that he should not pay more than $70. Moreover, the regular e-mail discounts make it clear that the customer would be foolish to buy anything from Banana Republic that is not on sale at a significant discount. As a result, although the retailer may experience a bump in sales during promotional periods, this approach also substantially reduces the lifetime value of its customers.

That is not to say that retailers should never have sales or use price to promote their products. For example, when a new product is introduced, it might make sense for a company to employ a *market penetration strategy* to maximize its customer share before its competitors launch competing products. New razors are often sold this way, as the company plans to make its profit on the subsequent sale of blades. In contrast, some firms instead choose to introduce new products using a *skimming strategy* that launches at a high price point to maximize profits by selling the initial inventory to the customer segments willing to pay more. Electronics retailers and manufacturers often use this type of strategy with new gaming consoles, next-generation televisions, or similar products.

There will always be situations in which a company over-predicts demand or overestimates the value customers perceive in a product and needs to engage in markdowns to sell it. On other occasions, a company uses a sale to create excitement and generate store traffic – for example, during the launch of a new product or store. In some cases, high-low pricing can let the company increase its overall profitability by capturing differences in perceived value between customer segments – for example, it can charge consumers who desire up-to-the-minute fashions more than customers who are willing to wait for a sale. Nevertheless, retailers need to be careful about how much they rely on price discounts to drive revenue and be aware of the impact that too many promotions can have on consumers' perceptions of value.

Everyday Low Prices

In response to the dangers of high-low pricing, some retailers today run on systems that allow for a more consistent process of everyday low prices (EDLP). In EDLP, the retailer's price is lower than the regular price at a high-low store but higher than the discounted price of the same product on sale. In other words, the retailer offers a relatively low and fair price to consumers on a regular basis and only rarely engages in markdowns and sales. EDLP retailers often make low-price guarantees to prevent losing business to the discounts of high-low merchants. Everyday low pricing can reduce the often high costs associated with sales advertising and constantly changing prices. The real benefit, however, is the opportunity to build relationships with consumers by assuring them that they are purchasing products at a fair price. In addition, EDLP can simplify inventory management by making year-over-year demand more predictable – because the large peaks and valleys created by sales promotions are flattened out – which helps to minimize stock-outs and ensure that customers can find the products they desire. Overall, when well executed, EDLP allows retailers to focus less on price competition and more on the long-term value of their customer base.

Although EDLP is increasingly popular, it has two major impediments. The first is the cost structure of the organization. If a company has a cost structure that results in perpetually higher prices or lower margins than its competition, an EDLP strategy tends to have a negative impact on the firm's value. For example, small local stores that sell the same products as large global retailers may have substantially higher inventory costs because they cannot buy in the same volume. Similarly, unionized retailers may have higher labor costs than their non-union competitors. In the long run, companies with higher costs tend to either fail or find ways to be more competitive – for example, by joining buying groups or negotiating more competitive employment contracts. As a retailer's costs fall, an EDLP approach becomes a more viable strategy.

The second major impediment to the adoption of a strict EDLP strategy is the concern that too much money is left on the table when the company fails to match its prices closely to consumers' perceptions of value and willingness to pay. In other words, an EDLP approach looks at value in the aggregate and does not account for differences between segments or individuals. For example, consider the price that Regal Entertainment Group charges for movie tickets. The company could use an EDLP strategy and charge a flat rate for all shows at any time; however, it would have empty theaters during the week and be turning customers away on the weekend. In addition, it would have to spend more money on renovations because all customers would want to watch movies in 3-D, RPX, Regal Recliners, and IMAX theaters with the biggest screens and the most advanced technology. Regal would also risk losing the more price-sensitive family and senior segments, who might choose to watch a movie at home or spend their leisure time elsewhere.

However, by charging more for popular show times and better viewing environments and less to children and seniors, Regal increases the number of customers it serves. As a result, the company enjoys greater revenue and profitability than it could with EDLP.

Dynamic Pricing

In general, the approach to pricing used by companies like Regal is referred to as price discrimination or dynamic pricing. The basic idea is to capture the value that increasingly small segments of consumers perceive in the product offering. In fact, when consumer marketers talk about dynamic pricing, they are really talking about charging each individual customer the maximum price they are willing to pay for a product. Airlines operate some of the most advanced dynamic pricing systems. For example, American Airlines changes its prices across all of its planes and routes more than one hundred thousand times each day in an attempt to fill every seat at the highest possible price. A lot of the early hype around online consumer auctions at sites like eBay was driven by the fact that the bidding process extracted the maximum price from shoppers – the "winner" of the auction was willing to pay more than anyone else.

Yet, as attractive as dynamic pricing is in theory, several companies have found substantial consumer resistance to it. In a now classic example, Coca-Cola learned this lesson the hard way when it introduced vending machines that, according to an article in the *New York Times*, varied the price of a soft drink based on factors such as the weather and consumer demand at a particular location.[10] Coca-Cola knew that, in hot weather, demand for a cola was much higher and consumers placed greater value on convenient access to an ice-cold drink. The vending machine included a temperature sensor to gauge the weather and a computer chip to determine the change in price. From the company's perspective, this was only the beginning. For the future, Coca-Cola envisaged generations of smart vending machines able to adjust prices based on several other factors that the company believed affected consumers' willingness to pay. For example, during hours of the day that drinking Coke was less popular, such as early in the morning, the vending machine would sell soft drinks at lower prices. Similarly, if the drinks sold quickly from a particular machine, or only a few cans were left, the price could increase to reflect the high level of consumer demand. Theoretically, these vending machines allowed the company to use its knowledge of its customers' preferences and purchase be-havior to better match the value customers perceived in the product to the price they were being charged. Coca-Cola and the vending ma-chine industry saw this as a positive innovation that was very similar to the dynamic pricing systems used by companies such as American Airlines and Regal theaters.

What Coca-Cola failed to anticipate was the consumer reaction to the *New York Times* story. People were upset with the idea of being charged different prices from the same machine based on factors that were be-yond their control. The same day that the article appeared, Coca-Cola claimed that the press reports were inaccurate and that it would not introduce machines that varied the price based on the weather. Nev-ertheless, other newspaper articles and blog posts began to criticize the company for trying to take advantage of consumers and to mock the idea that customers would now have to negotiate with a vending machine to purchase a soft drink. Clearly, something about a vending machine that engaged in temperature-based dynamic pricing did not sit right with people.

Yet, the price of a can of Coke can vary dramatically depending on when and where it is purchased. A guest at a luxury hotel might pay six or seven dollars for a can of Coke delivered by room service. If that same guest made the effort to find one of the hotel's vending machines, he might pay only a couple of dollars. If the hotel were located across the street from a convenience store, he could cross the street and pay less than a dollar. At home he would probably be able to buy a dozen cans from the grocery store for less than fifty cents each. Would people be as upset if the grocery store raised its prices during the hot summer months and put Coke on sale during a cold winter day?

Amazon has also earned the ire of customers who have accused it of engaging in dynamic pricing. In one example, a journalist reported that he put a relatively obscure book into his shopping cart and when he returned to buy it the next day the price had increased.[11] Wondering if this was just a coincidence, he added several books to his shopping cart and returned to find that many of them had increased in price. In a similar incident, Amazon faced an uproar over its DVD sales when some consumers believed it was basing prices on customer loyalty. Specifically, it appeared that the company was using data on individual customers' online shopping patterns to charge higher prices to loyal customers who did not price shop.[12] Amazon responded that the price discrepancies were not the result of systematic price discrimination but were instead the result of a limited test on the impact price has on purchasing patterns. In any case, the company was left with high-profile negative publicity and some very dissatisfied customers.

To understand why people get so upset with dynamic pricing by companies like Coke and Amazon, it is helpful to consider the results of research by behavioral economists into the way humans tend to play the ultimatum game. In the ultimatum game, two players must divide a sum of money – for example, $10. One player, the "proposer," offers the other, the "responder," some portion of the $10, from $0 up to the entire $10. The responder can either accept the offer or reject it. If the responder accepts it, the money is split between the two players as proposed. For example, if the responder accepts the proposed offer of $4, the responder keeps $4 and the proposer walks away with $6. The catch, however, is that if the responder rejects the offer, neither player is allowed to keep anything. From a rational perspective, the responder should accept any positive offer – even $1 – because rejecting the offer means gaining nothing. In fact, one might argue that the responder should accept even an offer of $0 because she or he is no worse off than before the offer was made. However, across a large number of studies with different amounts of money and players from a variety of cultures, the results are consistent: proposers offer 40 to 50 percent of the total amount of money, and responders reject offers below 30 percent.[13]

Clearly, players do not only consider their own payoff in the game and are ready to sacrifice their own gains to punish those who they believe are acting unfairly. In fact, fairness plays a critical role in both the ultimatum game and consumers' reaction to dynamic pricing systems. Generally, customers viewed weather-driven vending machines and DVD sales based on loyalty as unfair pricing schemes, and reacted vehemently. In the case of Regal Entertainment Group, people are more willing to accept that, given a fixed number of seats, it is fair to charge more for better technology and preferred viewing times. In the airline industry, consumers are used to the way in which prices vary, even if they are not always happy with the process.

Dynamic pricing requires technology that has only recently been widely available. As a result, retailers are really just beginning to think about and experiment with systems that can match price to perceived value for individual customers across a large range of products. Nevertheless, the initial case studies from companies like Coke and Amazon, as well as more academic research examining the underlying drivers of consumer decisions, indicate that for many people fairness can be a more important consideration than economic gain. As a result, in many situations retailers are likely to be more successful in the long run by ensuring that their pricing policies are perceived to be fair by their target segments, even if that means sacrificing some of the gains that may be achieved in the short run through dynamic pricing.

Checking Out the Competition

Part of what makes pricing such a difficult task is that even after a retailer meticulously develops a strategy and implements it with exacting precision, the competition can derail it. Each of the general pricing strategies I have discussed in this chapter can easily fail if the retailer is not able to adapt in response to competitors' actions. For example, a well-designed cost-based approach built on an average markup that both customers and the retailer have been happy with in the past will struggle when it leads to substantially higher prices than those an aggressive new competitor is offering. Similarly, an EDLP policy that consistently produces prices above those of the competition will find it hard to attract customers. If a retailer's high-low strategy results in consistently high prices when the competition is low, the company will only attract customers when its products are on sale and the revenue it generates will have minimal profitability.

Therefore, successful retailing requires both a strong general pricing strategy consistent with the overall retail value proposition and also the ability to adapt to competitors. Once again, knowing one's customers can be extremely helpful when it comes time to react to competitors' pricing decisions. Not all customers are aware of competitors' prices, and not all customers are willing to switch to a different store based on price alone. If a retailer has a limited knowledge of its own customers, then it can only respond to competitive actions through general markdowns that hurt overall profitability. However, if the retailer has a deeper understanding of its customers' price sensitivity and propensity to switch stores at an individual or small-segment level, then it can reach out to only customers at risk.

To avoid the complexity of a well-designed pricing strategy, many smaller retailers use a simpler copycat approach – that is, they set prices based on what others charge for similar items. Retailers that take this *price matching* approach emphasize the ESE components of the retail value proposition. In practical terms, this is also what large retailers do with their price matching guarantees: they are saying, "You do not need to focus on price when you shop with us because we will not be undersold." In general, as the level of retail competition continues to increase, retailers need to continue to ensure that they have fair prices. However, as it becomes more difficult to differentiate on price alone, success and failure are increasingly determined by the skill with which managers are able to command the ESE components when crafting a retail value proposition.

Chapter Twelve

Propositions: Pitfalls and Potential

F.W. Woolworth was the original global low-price retailer. The company got its start when Frank Winfield Woolworth opened his "Great Five Cent Store" in Lancaster, Pennsylvania, in 1879. Woolworths focused on delivering value to its customers. Selection was a major source of competitive advantage as Frank scoured Europe for products that would be exclusive to Woolworths. The company put pressure on prices and often undercut the competition to build market share and grow the chain of what came to be known as "Five and Ten Cent" stores across the United States, Canada, and into the United Kingdom. As his obituary said, "He made his money not by selling a little for a lot, but by selling a lot for a little."[1]

The company set new standards for global growth and revenue expansion. Woolworths was a cherished institution for many shoppers in the United States, Canada, and the United Kingdom. In 1913, the Woolworth building, which has become an iconic part of Manhattan's architecture and skyline, was completed in New York City. Frank paid for the $13.5 million construction in cash, and it was the tallest building in the world until the Chrysler building was erected in 1930.

In 1979, on Woolworths' 100th anniversary, *the Guinness Book of Records* recognized the retailer as the largest in the world. The company had created a new category of discount retailing and a model of doing business focused on price and product that became commonplace on main streets across the country. Walmart began with Walton's Five and Dime store in Bentonville based on the basic concept that Woolworths had built into a global phenomenon.

Nevertheless, after one hundred years in business its competitors were growing in stature and gaining market share. The company struggled through the 1980s and by the late 1990s Woolworths closed up shop in the United States and Canada. In 2009 the U.K. stores closed their doors for the last time. Like many of the retail stories and anecdotes in this book, the history of Woolworths illustrates how difficult it is to create and maintain success in retailing. When in 1979 Woolworths was being recognized as the world's most successful retailer, Sam Walton was in the early stages of expanding his business. Competitors like T.J. Maxx were still struggling to find their footing, and Costco was yet to open its first store. Retail is a tough business. There is no magic bullet or simple recipe for success.

Proposition Pitfalls

The approach to crafting a retail value proposition presented in this book puts the customer at the center of the strategic planning process. It is a framework that provides an integrative process for thinking about the customer experience in terms of three components – environment, selection, and engagement – that are evaluated by consumers relative to the price being charged. Each chapter has introduced several measures that retailers can use to track and evaluate their progress, as well as to inform forward-looking managerial decisions. This approach has been built on insights gleaned from hundreds of hours in conversation with retailers, supported by a large body of academic research, and illustrated with a variety of different retail examples and case studies. Those conversations, research papers, and case studies also reveal four common pitfalls that prevent retailers from realizing the full potential of their value propositions.

Believing in Best Practices

Best practices in designing shopping environments, managing product selections, and building engaging customer relationships can inform the development of a retailer's value proposition. Throughout this book, I have used case studies and retail anecdotes to illustrate key points related to crafting a value proposition. Now comes the caveat.

Success in retail is in the details of putting the individual components of a strategic position together – simply adopting what has worked for others is not sufficient. Every main street in America had a version of the five-and-dime retail store, but only Sam Walton was able to build the heir to the Woolworths legacy and create not just the world's largest retailer but the world's largest company, period. Similarly, for many years, companies around the world worked to emulate the processes and procedures that made Toyota such an admired and successful company. There is much to be learned from what Toyota has accomplished, just as retailers can learn from industry leaders like Home Depot and Target. However, GM cannot build its business by being like Toyota because the two companies have different corporate histories, cultures, labor agreements, dealer networks, product lines, and customer relationships. While GM may be able to learn from Toyota, to be successful it must craft its own unique value proposition at prices that are both compelling for customers and profitable for the company. Similarly, Target needs to manage its offering to compete with Walmart, just as Lowe's has to carve out its own unique market position relative to Home Depot. These companies can learn from each other and, as a result, the retail industry will continue to become more sophisticated and efficient. Ultimately, however, a retailer's success is determined not by what it does that makes it the same as its competitors but by what it does differently – that is, how the company puts the ESE components together with compelling prices to create a *unique* value proposition.

Confusing Price with Value

Perceived value is a combination of the consumer experience – as defined by shopping environment, product selection, and customer engagement – and the price the retailer charges. From the customer's perspective, value increases when the experience is held constant and prices fall, or when prices are held constant and the experience improves. In a competitive market, perceived value also depends on the competition. If the consumer experience declines relative to the competition, then to maintain the perceived value of its offering a retailer must drop its prices by an equivalent amount. However, if the retailer improves its consumer experience relative to the competition, then it can increase prices to reflect its superior offering. To a large extent this is where Woolworths lost its way. The original five-and-dime model was being replaced by very low cost local discount stores and very efficient supercenters and warehouse clubs that offered more to consumers at the same or lower prices. Woolworths was still doing what it did very well, but the expectations of consumers changed as competitors were able to improve the overall value they were offering.

Crafting a unique value-enhancing customer experience takes a great deal of time, effort, and investment. From the retailer's perspective, it is easier to increase the perceived value of its offering by cutting the price. That is not always a bad thing. The value that consumers perceive in an offering can change quickly and can vary substantially across segments or even individuals. In the short term, it often makes sense for a retailer to adapt to market conditions through price adjustments. In the long term, however, the focus should be on enhancing the customer experience – that is where competitive advantage is created. As I discussed in chapter 11, competing on price alone is a dangerous strategic position that puts tremendous pressure on both revenue and profitability. As retailers become increasingly sophisticated and efficient, the ability to differentiate on price is ever more difficult, even for the world's largest volume retailers.

In addition, when a retailer lowers its price, it signals to consumers that the offer is of less value. In recent years, North American automobile companies have struggled with this problem. For example, GM introduced a discount program that gave consumers an "employee discount" on new cars that was wildly successful in producing sales – at the lower price points, consumers saw the increased value in GM vehicles relative to the competition.[2] The problem was, the discounts also convinced consumers that there was no need to pay a premium for a GM vehicle. The perceived value of a GM vehicle decreased from the consumers' perspective, and at regular prices sales slowed dramatically.

Mismanaging Marketing

GM is not alone in its focus on the short term. In part, the blame falls on marketers who have not been accountable to the bottom line. Under the banner of "brand building" or "traffic generation," many different retailers have spent money on advertising campaigns and price discounting promotions with only an ambiguous notion of return on investment. The marketing department, like the rest of a retail organization, needs to be accountable to financial performance. Sustainable profitability depends on a strong overall value proposition. Today's consumers are sophisticated shoppers armed with a historically unprecedented volume of accessible information. It is a mistake to believe that advertising alone can create value for consumers.[3] Advertising can help to make consumers aware of the value a retailer offers, but it is not a substitute for a compelling value proposition. Rather than designing campaigns to generate short-term sales, the role of marketing within a retail organization should extend beyond advertising and promotions to a central role in the value creation process.

Minding the Store, Forgetting the Customers

The ESE components of the value proposition are all essential ingredients for retail success. Obviously, a retailer cannot operate for very long without a location – whether a physical store or an electronic one. Without a selection of products, retailers would have nothing to sell. Nevertheless, putting the shopping environment and product selection before the customer is a common mistake. In each chapter in this book, I have emphasized the importance of being customer-centric. In practice, however, the shopping environment and the product assortment are the tangible elements of retail management. Customers are more difficult to understand. They do not come with engineering or manufacturing specifications. They are not created to accommodate the retailer's systems or processes. They come in many shapes and sizes, with individual preferences that change over time, and their spending decisions can be dramatically influenced by seemingly irrelevant factors (such as who else is in the aisle with them,[4] or the amount of daily sunlight).[5] In other words, the customer is, to a large extent, out of the manager's control. There is never enough solid information and, as a result, decisions about customers have to be made under substantial uncertainty.

In contrast, managers have a great deal of control over the design of the shopping environment. Products come neatly packaged from manufacturers who make an effort to be as convenient and predictable as possible. Even the computer systems that underlie customer relationship management and consumer loyalty programs are built on a logical framework. The problem, of course, is that retailers do not make any money from the environment, products, or loyalty programs – the money comes from customers. That is what makes retailing so exciting. It is an unpredictable business that requires leaders to make major decisions with incomplete information and to adapt based on the response of the targeted consumer segments. It is a challenging business, but also one of tremendous potential.

The Potential

In practice, there are as many different value propositions as there are retailers, but the most successful companies constantly evolve to meet their customers' demands and desires. Bernie Marcus and Arthur

Blank's original vision for Home Depot was an enormous warehouse store that offered large selections and low prices to appeal to consumers. Over time, the company evolved to focus less on price and more on customer relationships. In addition, the company moved away from warehouse-style hardware stores designed for the do-it-yourself handyman and toward more female-friendly home improvement stores. Ganz integrated the old business of plush animals with new media and introduced the youngest consumers to the future of augmented reality. Lululemon grew rapidly from its humble beginnings as a Vancouver yoga apparel retailer into a global phenomenon built on the power of product innovation and community-based customer engagement. Costco created a business model that is driven by membership fees, which are in turn the result of a growing portfolio of customers loyal to its eclectic product mix. Tesco demonstrates the power of a loyalty program that uses the customer data it collects to enhance its value proposition. Macy's and Walgreen's were part of the early years of commerce in America and remain relevant more than 100 years later.

These retailers, and the many other companies profiled in this book, have played a leading role in shaping the retail industry in the United States and around the world. Each has crafted its own unique value proposition, which has evolved over time in response to economic cycles, increasingly intense competition, and changes in consumers' preferences. There is no single dominant approach. While Walmart has built the world's largest company (in terms of revenue) by focusing on price and product selection, Apple has become the world's most valuable company (in terms of market valuation) through product innovation and exceptional customer engagement.

Although there is little doubt that a strong modern economy needs retailers like Walmart and Apple, the future of retail is in small independent stores. Individually they have a negligible impact on the economy, but in aggregate they are the fast-moving entrepreneurial machine that drives innovation, job creation, and economic development. It may seem as though large global retail organizations have become so powerful and sophisticated that there is little opportunity for new retailers to survive, let alone thrive. Nevertheless, not so long ago, Woolworths was a dominant retailer that led the industry with creative innovations, intense price competitiveness, and a passionately loyal customer base. Only a few decades ago, companies like Kmart and Handy Dan Home Improvement were giants in their respective markets and dismissed Walmart and Home Depot as regional players unlikely to succeed in bigger markets.

Today, as retail competition focuses on customer engagement, the large retail chains spend billions of dollars in an attempt to better understand their customers. In essence, they are trying to replicate the strength of local independent stores that know their customers on a personal level. Successful small retailers do not need the same sort of sophisticated systems to help them design customer-centric environments and product selections because they know the segments they serve intimately and focus their operations on what their customers want.

Ultimately, regardless of the size of the store, successful retailing is not about offering lower prices than Walmart or besting Disney World's customer experience. It is not necessary to have the real estate of a Starbucks, Costco's product selection, or Tesco's Clubcard. The key to retail success is creating value for consumers by crafting unique experiences at compelling prices. Whether you are an aspiring merchant or an industry veteran, the retail value proposition is a solid foundation from which to build your business in today's perpetually evolving and increasingly competitive retail marketplace.

Acknowledgments

The roots of this book go back to mopping floors and facing shelves in my father's northern Alberta drug store – it was there that I fell in love with retailing. For that, and so much more, I have my family to thank.

This book began when Professor Michael Pearce walked into my office at the Richard Ivey School of Business and asked me if I would be interested in taking over his highly acclaimed and very popular undergraduate and MBA courses in retail management. I was both honored and intimidated by the opportunity, but Michael made it easy for me and I was hooked. Teaching that course eventually led to my current role as a professor of marketing and the director of the School of Retailing at the University of Alberta's School of Business – and, ultimately, to my writing this book.

Admittedly, I underestimated the time and effort required to write a book, and I am grateful for the encouragement and support of my wife, Colleen, even when the manuscript took over my evenings and weekends. As a thoughtful reader, constructive critic, and wonderful partner, Colleen has always made my projects our projects, for which I am eternally and happily in her debt.

I also truly appreciate the guidance of my editor, Jennifer DiDomenico, who with patience and a light touch has walked me through the process of publishing my first book.

Many people shaped my thinking about retail management over the years, and they deserve my thanks. My academic friends and mentors in the world of retailing – especially Adam Finn, Harmen Oppewal, Mike Percy, Dilip Soman, and Mark Vandenbosch – have always encouraged me to pursue my applied interests alongside more abstract and theoretical research. That encouragement opened the door for me to work as a consultant, educator, and adviser with several remarkable companies, including General Motors, Industry Canada, Johnson and Johnson, Leger Marketing, Loyalty-One, Microsoft, and Safeway. I have learned a great deal from my interactions with each of these organizations.

In recent years, I have benefited enormously from the opportunity to discuss retailing in North America and around the world with colleagues at the Dublin Institute of Technology and the Faculty of Business and Economics at Monash University. Their perspectives have broadened my own thinking on the global marketplace, and they have illuminated several interesting differences among English-speaking consumers in markets with a shared history. At the University of Alberta, my research assistant, Jonathan Lai, has been invaluable in helping me discover new resources and sources for the revised edition of the book.

I also want to thank my retail case co-authors including Jason Chan, Ramasastry Chandrasekhar, Miranda Goode, Jianping Liang, Ken Mark, Mike Moffat, Krista Morrison, Fabrizio Di Muro, and of course Michael Pearce. The cases and technical notes that we wrote together added greatly to my understanding of how retailers – including Acura, Apple, BMW, Home Depot, Indigo, Jill's Table, OQOQO/lululemon, Sears, and Sunripe Marketplace – operate in the real world.

As director of the University of Alberta's School of Retailing, I have been very fortunate to spend time with several of Canada's leading retail managers and executives. In particular, I have learned a great deal from the school's recent retail award winners: Wynne Powell (CEO, London Drugs), Chip Wilson (founder, lululemon), Annette Verschuren (former CEO, Home Depot Canada), Brian Hill (CEO, Aritzia), Mark Wolverton (CEO, LUSH Cosmetics), and Heather Reisman (CEO, Indigo). I greatly appreciate the one-on-one time that these world-class business leaders have spent with me, as well as the many hours they have given to our school and our students. Similarly, I have benefited enormously from the advice and guidance offered by the Retail Council of Canada and, in particular, the RCC's CEO, Diane Brisebois.

Of course, a lot of the most interesting and influential discussions I have had about retail were not in the classroom or in the boardroom or at an awards dinner but instead took place during a casual lunch or over a cup of coffee (often during a break at one of those more formal events). There have been many of those conversations over the years, and I know that as I try to compile a list I am regrettably forgetting some that should be included, for which I apologize.

Nevertheless, for their time, insight, advice, and wisdom, I want to thank Rob Bennet (ATB), Rob Britton (American Airlines), Jack Brown (J. Brown Group), Bill Campbell (Canada Safeway), David Cosco (Integra Tire), Kevin Higa (Running Room), Kim Irving (ATB), Larry Jenkinson (United Cycle), Edward Kennedy (The North West Company), Jean-Marc Leger (Leger Marketing), Clint Mahlman (London Drugs), Roy Martin (PepsiCo), Steve Matyas (Staples), Michael McLarney (Hardlines), Craig Patterson (Retail Inisder), Bryan Pearson (Loyalty-One), Bruce Reid (The Brick), Dave Rodych (Canada Safeway), Mark Ryski (HeadCount), Emily Salsbury (University of Alberta, School of Retailing), and Graeme Young (Avison Young Commercial Real Estate).

Grateful thanks also go to the three institutions that have enthusiastically supported my research – the Richard Ivey School of Business at Ontario's Western University, the Faculty of Business and Economics at Monash University, and the Alberta School of Business at the University of Alberta. Finally, I would like to acknowledge and thank my students, who continually impress me with their intellectual curiosity, novel insights, and passion for retailing.

Notes

Chapter 1

1 Barbara Thau, "Apple and the Other Most Successful Retailers by Sales per Square Foot," *Forbes* (20 May 2014). Accessed 3 July 2015: http://www.forbes.com/sites/barbarathau/2014/05/20/apple-and-the-other-most-successful-retail-stores-by-sales-per-square-foot/.

2 Jennifer Reingold, "How to Fail in Business While Really, Really Trying," *Fortune.com*, 20 March 2014. Accessed 3 July 2015: http://fortune.com/2014/03/20/how-to-fail-in-business-while-really-really-trying/.

3 Ibid.

4 Taylor Clark, *Starbucked: A Double Tall Tale of Caffeine, Commerce, and Culture* (New York: Back Bay Books, 2007).

5 Ibid.

6 C.C. Williams, "Rethinking the Role of the Retail Sector in Economic Development," *Service Industries Journal* 17, no. 2 (1997): 205–20; and C.C. Williams, *Consumer Services and Economic Development* (New York: Routledge, 1997).

7 R. Debanjali, *Retail Services: Measure and Contribution to National Income* (PhD diss., University of Miami, 2008: http://scholarlyrepository.miami.edu/oa_dissertations/133/).

Chapter 2

1 "LCBO Corporate Timeline." Accessed 17 February 2016: http://www.lcbo.com/content/lcbo/en/corporate-pages/about/media-centre/corporate-timeline.html#.VsSewsf1d_c.

2 "LCBO's Brandt Pours on Results," *Strategy*, 16 July 2001: http://strategyonline.ca/2001/07/16/lcbo-20010716.
3 Ibid.
4 Ibid.
5 Malcom Gladwell, *What the Dog Saw and Other Adventures* (New York: Little, Brown and Company, 2009).

Chapter 3

1 John W. Reilly, *Law of Retail Gravitation* (New York: published by author, 1931).
2 Ibid.
3 This is not to suggest that $500 should be a sales-per-square-foot target for a new store, but simply to illustrate how a retailer might project sales in a new store based on the prior performance of a similar store in another location.
4 Gayle Soucek, *Marshall Field's: The Store That Helped Build Chicago* (Charleston, SC: The History Press, 2010).
5 Ibid.

Chapter 4

1 Nitin Nohria and Bridget Gurtler, "Clarence Saunders: The Comeback King," Harvard Business School Case #9–404–070, May 2004 (revised July 2004).
2 Piggly Wiggly, "About Us," last updated 2011: http://www.pigglywiggly.com/about-us.
3 Paco Underhill, *Why We Buy: The Science of Shopping* (New York: Simon & Schuster, 1999), 31.
4 Jeffrey J. Inman, Russell S. Winer, and Rosellina Ferraro, "The Interplay among Category Characteristics, Customer Characteristics, and Customer Activities on In-Store Decision Making," *Journal of Marketing* 73, no. 5 (May 2009): 19–29.
5 Ibid.
6 Herb Sorensen, *Inside the Mind of the Shopper* (Upper Saddle River, NJ: Wharton School Publishing, 2009).
7 Underhill, *Why We Buy*.
8 Inman, Winer, and Ferraro, "The Interplay among Category Characteristics, Customer Characteristics, and Customer Activities on In-Store Decision Making."

9 Raymond R. Burke, "Technology and the Customer Interface: What Consumers Want in the Physical and Virtual Store," *Journal of the Academy of Marketing Science* 30, no. 4 (2002): 411–32.
10 Sorensen, *Inside the Mind of the Shopper.*
11 Jeffrey S. Larson, Eric T. Bradlow, and Peter S. Fader, "How Do Shoppers Really Shop?" *ECR Journal* 6, no. 1 (2006): 56–63.
12 Inman, Winer, and Ferraro, "The Interplay among Category Characteristics, Customer Characteristics, and Customer Activities on In-Store Decision Making."
13 Sorensen, *Inside the Mind of the Shopper.*
14 Kyle B. Murray, Fabrizio F. Di Muro, Adam Finn, and Peter Popkowski Leszczyc, "The Effect of Weather on Consumer Spending," *Journal of Retailing and Consumer Services* 17, no. 6 (2010): 512–20.
15 Ibid.
16 Kordelia Spies, Frederick Hesse, and Kerstin Loesch, "Store Atmosphere, Mood, and Purchasing Behavior," *International Journal of Research in Marketing* 14 (February 1997): 1–17.
17 Underhill, *Why We Buy*, 61.
18 Sanjay K. Dhar and Stephen J. Hoch, "Price Discrimination Using In-Store Marketing," *Journal of Marketing* 60, no. 1 (January 1996): 17–30.
19 Sam K. Hui, Peter S. Fader, and Eric T. Bradlow, "The Travelling Salesman Goes Shopping: The Systematic Deviations of Grocery Paths from TSP Optimality," *Marketing Science* 28, no. 3 (May 2009): 566–72.
20 Inman, Winer, and Ferraro, "The Interplay among Category Characteristics, Customer Characteristics, and Customer Activities on In-Store Decision Making."

Chapter 5

1 Cindy Liu, "Worldwide Retail Ecommerce: The eMarketer Forecast for 2015," *eMarketer* (2015).
2 PewResearchCenter: Internet, Science & Tech, "Internet Use over Time." Accessed 22 July 2015: http://www.pewinternet.org/data-trend/internet-use/internet-use-over-time/.
3 Ibid.
4 eMarketer, "Comparative Estimates: US Fixed Broadband Households and Penetration, 2013–2017," *eMarketer.com* (August 2014).
5 Statista, "Number of Monthly Active Facebook Users Worldwide as of 1st Quarter 2015 (in millions)." Accessed 27 July 2015: http://www.statista.com/statistics/264810/number-of-monthly-active-facebook-users-worldwide/.

6 eMarketer, "US Facebook Users and Penetration, 2013–2019," *eMarketer. com* (February 2015).

7 James Cook, "After Selling for $850 Million, Failed Social Network Bebo Is Relaunching as Something Much Cooler," *Business Insider* (10 December 2014). Accessed 27 July 2015: http://www.businessinsider.com/bebo-is-relaunching-as-a-chat-app-2014-12.

8 Jeff Beer, "The New Dot-Com Boom," *Canadian Business* (14 February 2011): 28–34. Accessed 27 July 2015: http://www.canadianbusiness.com/technology-news/outlook-2011-the-new-dot-com-boom/.

9 Ibid.

10 Alistair Barr and Clare Baldwin, "Groupon's IPO Biggest by US Web Company since Google," *Reuters* (4 November 2011).

11 Joan Lappin, "Don't Cry for Groupon's Andrew Mason," *Forbes* (3 May 2013). Accessed 27 July 2015: http://www.forbes.com/sites/joanlappin/2013/03/05/dont-cry-for-groupons-andrew-mason/.

12 David Kushner, "Webkinz Effect: Plush-Toy Fad Begets Imitators," *Wired* 16, no. 11 (20 October 2008). Accessed 27 July 2015: http://www.wired.com/2008/10/st-webkinz/.

13 eMarketer, "Leading Grocery Websites among UK Online Buyers, 2008," *eMarketer.com*, last updated 2008: http://www.emarketer.com.

14 Macy's Inc., "Refinement of M.O.M. Strategies." Accessed 27 July 2015: http://macysinc.com/macys/m.o.m.-strategies/default.aspx.

15 Alexis Madrigal, "How Netflix Reverse Engineered Hollywood," *The Atlantic* (2 January 2014). Accessed 27 July 2014: http://www.theatlantic.com/technology/archive/2014/01/how-netflix-reverse-engineered-hollywood/282679/.

Chapter 6

1 Leslie Kaufman, "Shares of Gap Fall after Chief Executive Calls It Quits," *New York Times*, 22 May 2002.

2 Tina Gaudoin, "Mickey Drexler: Retail Therapist," *Magazine from the Wall Street Journal*, 10 June 2010.

3 Ibid.

4 Meryl Gordon, "Mickey Drexler's Redemption," *New York Magazine*, 21 May 2005.

5 Michael R. Pearce, "Note on Retail Assortment," Richard Ivey School of Business Technical Note #9B05A035, 2005.

6 Steven D. Levitt and Stephen J. Dubner, *Freakonomics: A Rogue Economist Explores the Hidden Side of Everything* (New York: HarperCollins Publishers Inc., 2005).

7 Mark Borden, "Shaun White's Business Is Red Hot," *Fast Company*,
   1 February 2009.
8 Barbara Smit, *Sneaker Wars: The Enemy Brothers Who Founded Adidas and
   Puma and the Family Feud That Forever Changed the Business of Sport*
   (New York: HarperCollins Publishers Inc., 2008).
9 ACNielsen, *The State of Private Label around the World 2014: Where It's Growing,
   Where It's Not and What the Future Holds* (New York: ACNielsen, 2014).
10 Ibid.
11 Ibid.
12 Nirmalya Kumar and Jan-Benedict E.M. Steenkamp, *Private Label Strategy:
   How to Meet the Store Brand Challenge* (Cambridge, MA: Harvard Business
   Review Press, 2007).
13 Ibid.
14 Nielsen, *The State of Private Label around the World*.
15 Roland T. Rust, Valerie A. Zeithaml, and Katherine A. Lemon, "Customer-
   Centered Brand Management," *Harvard Business Review* 82, no. 9
   (September 2004): 110–18.
16 Jack Neff, "Walmart Reversal Marks Victory for Brands," *Ad Age*, 22 March
   2010.

Chapter 7

1 ACNielsen, *Consumer-Centric Category Management: How to Increase Profits
   by Managing Categories Based on Consumers' Needs* (Hoboken, NJ: John
   Wiley & Sons, 2005).

Chapter 8

1 Caesar's Entertainment, "Company Information," last updated 2012:
   http://www.reviewjournal.com/business/casinos-gaming/harrahs-
   entertainment-becomes-caesars-entertainment-corp.
2 Caesar's Entertainment, "An Emergent Model in a Recovering Industry"
   (presentation, 2011 UBS Leveraged Finance Conference, May 2011).
3 Ibid.
4 Christina Binklet, "Lucky Numbers: Casino Chain Mines Data on Its
   Gamblers, and Strikes Pay Dirt," *Wall Street Journal*, 4 May 2000.
5 Frederick E. Webster, Alan J. Malter, and S. Ganesan, "The Decline and
   Dispersion of Marketing Competence," *MIT Sloan Management Review* 46,
   no. 4 (2005): 35–43.
6 Gary Loveman, "Diamonds in the Data Mine," *Harvard Business Review*,
   May 2003.

7 Ibid.
8 Barry Schwartz, *Paradox of Choice* (New York: HarperCollins Publishing Inc., 2005).
9 Claes Fornell, Sunil Mithas, Forrest V. Morgeson, III, and M.S. Krishnan, "Customer Satisfaction and Stock Prices: High Returns, Low Risk," *Journal of Marketing* 70 (January 2006): 3–14.
10 Herbert A. Simon, "A Behavioral Model of Rational Choice," *Quarterly Journal of Economics* 69, no. 1 (February 1955): 99–118.
11 George Stigler and Gary S. Becker, "De Gustibus Non Est Disputandum," *American Economic Review* 67, no. 2 (March 1977): 76–90.
12 John Crawley and David Bailey, "Toyota Chief to Testify before U.S. House Panel," *Reuters*, 18 February 2010.
13 Joel B. Cohen and Michael J. Houston, "Cognitive Consequences of Brand Loyalty," *Journal of Marketing Research* 9, no. 1(February 1972): 97–9.
14 Kyle B. Murray, "Small Equals Big Potential: The Value of Personal Service," *National Post, FP Executive*, 28 October 2008.
15 Gallup Consulting, *Employee Engagement: What's Your Engagement Ratio?* (Gallup Inc., 2010).
16 James K. Harter, Frank L. Schmidt, Emily A. Killham, and Sangeeta Agrawal, *Q12 Meta-Analysis: The Relationship between Engagement at Work and Organizational Outcomes* (Gallup Inc., 2009).

Chapter 9

1 Frederick F. Reichheld, "The One Number You Need to Grow," *Harvard Business Review*, December 2003.
2 Ibid.
3 Timothy L. Keiningham, Lerzan Aksoy, Bruce Cooil, and T. Wallin Andreassen, "Linking Customer Loyalty to Growth," *MIT Sloan Management Review*, Summer 2008.
4 Barnes & Noble, "Membership." Accessed 9 July 2015: http://www .barnesandnoble.com/membership/.
5 John A. McCarty and Manoj Hastak, "Segmentation Approaches in Data Mining: A Comparison of RFM, CHAID, and Logistic Regression," *Journal of Business Research* 60, no. 6 (June 2007): 656–62.
6 Roland T. Rust, Katherine N. Lemon, and Valerie A. Zeithaml, "Return on Marketing: Using Customer Equity to Focus Marketing Strategy," *Journal of Marketing* 68, no. 1 (January 2004): 109–27.
7 Jenny van Doorn and Peter C. Verhoef, "Critical Incidents and the Impact of Satisfaction on Customer Share," *Journal of Marketing* 72, no. 4 (July 2008): 123–42.

8 Ibid.
9 Terri Feldman Barr, David W. Rosenthal, and Thomas C. Boyd, "Starbucks Coffee: The Dorosin Issue (A)," *The Case Research Journal* (1998). Accessed 11 June 2012: http://starbucked.com/casestudy.html.

Chapter 10

1 Gary McWilliams, "The Customer Isn't Always Right: Best Buy Wants to Keep the Wrong Kind of Shopper Out of Its Stores," *Wall Street Journal: Classroom Edition*, January 2005: http://wsjclassroom.com/archive/05jan/bigb_bestbuy.htm.
2 Ibid.
3 Clive Humby, Terry Hunt, and Tim Phillips, *Scoring Points: How Tesco Continues to Win Customer Loyalty*, 2nd ed. (Philadelphia, PA: Kogan Page, 2007).
4 Consumer Intelligence Research Partners, "Amazon Prime Hits New Highs," *Analysis of Buyer Shopping Patterns for Amazon, Inc*, 27 January 2015.
5 John Maxfield, "Costco: The Membership Club That Also Happens to Be a Retailer," *The Motley Fool*, 23 June 2015: http://www.fool.com/investing/general/2015/06/23/costco-the-membership-club-that-also-happens-to-be.aspx. Accessed 25 June 2015.
6 Kelly Yamanouchi, "Hoarders Worry about the Fate of Their Frequent-Flier Miles," *Knight Ridder Tribune Business News*, 27 February 2005.
7 Kelly Klavinka and Jim Sullivan, *2011 Forecast of U.S. Consumer Loyalty Program Points Value* (Colloquy and Swift Exchange, 2011).
8 Grahame R. Dowling and Mark Uncles, "Do Customer Loyalty Programs Really Work?" *MIT Sloan Management Review* 38, no. 4 (Summer 1997): 71–82; Conor M. Henderson, Joshua T. Beck, and Robert W. Palmatier, "Review of the Theoretical Underpinnings of Loyalty Programs," *Journal of Consumer Psychology* 21 (July 2011): 257–73; Steven M. Shugan, "Brand Loyalty Programs: Are They Shams?" *Marketing Science* 24, no. 2 (Spring 2005): 185–93.
9 Humby, Hunt, and Phillips, *Scoring Points*.
10 Ibid.

Chapter 11

1 Andy Logan, "Double Darkness and Worst of All," *New Yorker*, 22 February 1958.
2 Elizabeth Periale, "Alexander Turney Stewart, Father of the Department Store," *Smithsonian Libraries* (blog), 14 September 2010: https://blog.library.si.edu/2010/09/alexander-turney-stewart/.

3 Ibid.

4 "Wal-Mart's Ad Slogan Changes after 19 Years," *Toronto Star*, 13 September 2007: http://www.thestar.com/business/2007/09/13/walmarts_ad_slogan_changes_after_19_years.html.

5 Daniel Kahneman and Amos Tversky, "The Framing of Decisions and the Psychology of Choice," *Science* 211, no. 4481 (30 January 1981): 453–8.

6 Richard Thaler, "Mental Accounting and Consumer Choice," *Marketing Science* 4, no. 3 (Summer 1985): 199–214.

7 Ibid., 206.

8 Shuba Srinivasan, "Do Promotions Benefit Manufacturers, Retailers, or Both?" *Management Science* 50, no. 5 (May 2004): 617–29.

9 Koen Pauwels, Jorge Silva-Risso, Shuba Srinivasan, and Dominique M. Hanssens, "New Products, Sales Promotions, and Firm Value: The Case of the Automobile Industry," *Journal of Marketing* 68, no. 4 (October 2004): 142–56.

10 Constance Hays, "Coke Tests Vending Unit That Can Hike Prices in Hot Weather," *New York Times*, 28 October 1999.

11 David Streitfeld, "Amazon Mystery: Pricing of Books," *LA Times*, 2 January 2007.

12 Craig Bicknell, "Online Prices Not Created Equal," *Wired*, 7 September 2000.

13 Martin A. Nowak, Karen M. Page, and Karl Sigmund, "Fairness versus Reason in the Ultimatum Game," *Science* 289, no. 8 (2000): 1773–5.

Chapter 12

1 Paul Seaton, "A Potted History of Woolworths Stores," *Woolworths Museum*, 2012. Accessed 13 July 2015: http://www.woolworthsmuseum.co.uk/aboutwoolies.html.

2 Barry J. Babin and Eric G. Harris, *CB2* (Mason, OH: South-Western, Cengage Learning, 2009).

3 Gerald J. Tellis, *Advertising Effectiveness: Understanding When, How and Why Advertising Works* (Thousand Oaks, CA: Sage Publications Inc., 2004).

4 Jennifer J. Argo, Darren W. Dahl, and Rajesh V. Manchanda, "The Influence of Mere Social Presence in a Retail Context," *Journal of Consumer Research* 32 (September 2005): 207–12.

5 Kyle Murray, Fabrizio Di Muro, Adam Finn, and Peter Popkowski Leszczyc, "The Effect of Weather on Consumer Spending," *Journal of Retailing and Consumer Services* 17 (2010): 512–20.

Index